M000083168

ANCESTOR PATHS

HONORING OUR ANCESTORS AND GUARDIAN SPIRITS THROUGH PRAYERS, RITUALS, AND OFFERINGS

A STEP BY STEP GUIDE

SECOND EDITION

Crystal Wise-Davis

BY

ALADOKUN

Copyright © 2009, 2012 by Oba Ilari Aladokun. All rights reserved. (Second Edition)

All rights reserved. No part of this publication may be reproduced, stored in a retrieval system, or transmitted, in any form or by any means, electronic, mechanical, photocopying, recording, or otherwise, without the written prior permission of the author.

IBSN-13: 978-0615648637
IBSN-10: 0615648630

Cover Design by Oba Ilari Aladokun

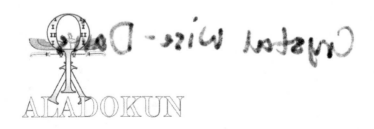

Ancestor Paths the Sequel
www.ancestorpaths.net
www.honor-ur-ancestors.com

ACKNOWLEDGMENTS

To Olodumare, Òrisànlá, the Òrìsà
and the Holy Ancestors

I give thanks to my elders and mentors,
Oluwo Ogunbayo and Iya Omitayo
for their continual prayers, guidance, and
correction each day, but also for the spiritual
support that opened the way for me to do
"Ancestors Paths, the Second Edition".

I give a personal thanks to Barry, for his
continued support and love in my life.
Through the ups & downs – you were there.
Thank you!

I give thanks to my beautiful mother &
daughter, for always being there.

I give thanks to my dearest friends & family,
mentors & teachers, who have encouraged
and inspired my growth and success.

And, to my students, supporters and readers,
I say, THANK YOU!

CONTENTS

TRIBUTE

My most important thank you is to Olodumare, God, my ancestors, and spirit guides, only because there are no words that could truly express how I feel. There are not enough thank yous in a lifetime that could say how much I am truly grateful and appreciative for the gifts, knowledge, and wisdom that they have bestowed upon me. I only pray that I can show them my many, many thanks by my continued efforts to share the gifts that have been given to me and to teach and share their knowledge and wisdom with the rest of the world. This was written for all those on the other side. I would also like to take this opportunity to say, *"we never know what cards we are going to be dealt in life or how we are going to play them. We may never know the reasons behind why things happen the way they do even though there is a reason for everything. We may be disillusioned by those around us because people are not who they appear to be. We may not always understand our choices, right or wrong; however, the outcome may be just how God intended it to be."*

I thank God and my superior guides for every experience, person, place, or thing that has influenced my life to make me the person that I am TODAY!

A SPECIAL DEDICATION

All praise, I give to, Òrisànlá, "Light of the World". Òrisànlá you are my Baba and the one who owns and crowns my head. Baba, you are the King of Kings and although many are attracted to your kingship, I only know you as my loving and protective father. Then I learned that you prefer it this way, for Fathers are loved and Kings are betrayed. So I only live to honor you.

Obàtálá, you give me light in my dark moments and without ritual or offering you come when I call to give me your strength to lean on. When I want to give up, you always find a way to push me through and I thank you.

Òrisànlá, like a true God, your patience with me is, oh so, welcoming as I walk this earth plane with many imperfections. Your compassion has never wavered during my trials and tribulations. Your forgiveness is unmatched and I thank you.

Mankind says, "You never know who your friends are until times are bad." I know you are not only my only my Baba, but my friend; the kind of friend that will never let me down and a friend that wants nothing but to hear my voice. Only you, Baba, can give and do for me in a way that no man nor woman can and I thank you for being there for me.

Obàtálá, because you shine, I shine. Your fame is my fame. Your light is my light. Your Àṣe is my Àṣe. Thank you for allowing me to do all the many special things that I do for myself and others. Thank you for allowing me to side track and learn about other spiritual approaches to healing and well-being. For sure, this has helped me to know you better because I know that you live in all those things.

Thank you for tolerating me and I ask your forgiveness if I have ever offended you during my times of anger, confusion, frustration, naivety, and rebellions. Obàtálá, I know that you are the God that walks with me, lives in me and works through me. To the best of my ability, I promise to walk this earth plane with the utmost respect, humility, and integrity that YOU exemplify.

Òrisànlá, you are one of my eldest ancestors and this book is a tribute and a testimony of your GLORY! I am grateful that this GLORY, your GLORY, walks with me to affect as many as possible. I only pray that all will know your GLORY as well as I do.

Àṣe o

I SURRENDER
By Oba Ilari Aladokun

I surrender my mind, my heart, and my soul over to the will of my ancestors, spirit guides/eguns, and the Òrìsà who exist within the universe, overseen by the creator, because I trust that they know what is best.

My creator and my guides will make everything right for me as long as I surrender willfully. I will allow the forces of nature and the essence of their power to flow through me like a river's stream, moving me in the direction that is most beneficial for my well-being.

I release and surrender willfully to accept the challenges placed before me, for I know that I exist because of—and I am at the disposal of—the Supreme Being and the universe. I have learned that resisting only creates conflicts, frustration, uncertainty, and chaos within myself, making me miserable, unhappy, and angry with the world; therefore, I will not worry, and I choose the path of least resistance on all levels of consciousness, for the universe will use me and place me where I need to be.

To ease my path through life, why fight? I will be moved by the universe whether I want to be or not; therefore, in the name of all that is holy, just, and pure in light, I SURRENDER!

FOREWORD

I wrote this book because I remember how hard it was trying to learn about ancestor/spirit and nature veneration from within the spiritual systems of Santeria/Lukumi. Santeria/Lukumi stemmed from the African Diaspora and is a derivative of the Afrikan religion Yoruba. *Wikipedia, The Free Encyclopedia* defines the Afrikan Diaspora as the movement of Afrikans and their descendants to places throughout the world—predominantly to the Amerikas, then later to Europe, the Middle East, and other corners of the globe. Much of the Afrikan Diaspora is descended from people who were enslaved and shipped to the Amerikas during the Atlantic slave trade.

From the time that I began my journey on the path of ancestor/spirit veneration through the past several years, information on this subject was limited, vague, and confusing. And even though today there is an abundance of information available from other books and the Internet, I still find most of it vague, confusing, and incomplete. Therefore, it is my goal to make the road a little easier for those who would like to grasp the concepts of ancestor/spirit veneration. To take the confusion out of the process, I created this step-by-step guide to help those who have no guidance but who need good and valid information to at least help themselves on their own journeys. I also wanted to write a book that would be easy to read and comprehend—with a little humanity added, too. This work is not all technical. In the end, it is deeply personal.

Taking a broad, non-discriminatory perspective, this book highlights the importance of ancestor veneration and spiritualism. Every human being has an ancestor. It doesn't matter who you are or where you come from; we can all relate to death on some level, and this keeps us connected whether we realize it or not. The primary purpose of this book is to help us maintain some sort of spiritual connection to nature, our ancestors and spirit guides for a better way of life. Whereas most people seek religion to be saved, I am offering people the opportunity to save themselves through guided spirituality and the connection to spirit. Although this work primarily touches on Afrikan spirituality, because this is my background—and I can only speak about what I know and my own experiences—it does not exclude other ethnic groups. The principles and techniques in this book can be applied to anyone with any issue, within any culture.

Ancestor veneration is totally misunderstood by millions because of misinterpreted, hidden, lost, and forgotten historical information about its true purpose and foundation. However, there are those who are familiar with its vision but have taken a relaxed attitude toward its importance. Either way, and in many cases, I believe that many of the problems that we suffer today in our families and in our communities— from mental illness, family dysfunction, verbal and physical abuse, drug addiction, violence, alcoholism, suicide, and other forms of self-destructive behaviors—can come from spirits, ancestors, or karmic connections to our loved ones or other spirit entities who have not been appeased or who, on some level, have not elevated into the light of God so that their souls can be at peace. And since they are not at peace, these entities cause us, in the living, to suffer within ourselves, in our families and in our communities, and as a result, we continue to experience social malice; psychic, mental and emotional confusion; and spiritual problems that in many cases are directly tied to the disassociation of not having properly taken care of these unsettled spirits and/or ancestors.

Ancestor Paths is a tribute to Òrisànlá who has paved the way for me. It is a tribute to the ones who have walked before me, to the ones whose blood runs through my veins, to the ones whom I remember, to the ones whose names and faces I do not know, and to the ones whom I have forgotten; it is a calling of their spirits in honor of their contributions and enduring presence that is always near us and with us. This tribute is a reminder to remember and preserve the memories of the past, for these memories will guide us through the present and unite and reunite us in the future. As long as we remember, our oppressors can never forget. It is through the ancestors that we are taught and reminded that we are a people born from predecessors of a proud culture. The richness of our heritage and the legacies left behind will remain forever alive, as long as we continue to call their names.

Ancestor Paths is also a tribute to all the divinities of the universe that continue to guide and bless me and us while elevating our souls toward higher evolution. And for all of us, *Ancestor Paths* is about commemorating the Creator, the ancestors, the spirit guides/eguns, and the Òrìsà, for without them, where would we be?

For me, each time we save a soul and help it elevate, this becomes one less spirit able to cause havoc in our families/communities and in the world.

I write and dedicate this work to all those on the other side.

SPIRT OF HOPE
by Sharon Black-Estella

*Oh, Divine Spirits of the Universe,
Today, we call upon the Spirit of Hope;
that small part of us which resounds
vibrantly when needed.*

*We bid welcome to the angels and guides
of my beloved family and friends who are
here to acknowledge the strength that the
Spirit of HOPE lights in all of us.*

*May we all be truly thankful that HOPE
lights our way through despair,
loneliness, and disappointments.*

*We seek this light, for each that reaps its
benefits and passes the message to
humanity.*

*We join forces with the Spirits of Wisdom
and Love to heal us, transform us, and
manifest the opening of closed doors.*

*Hope illuminates and dispatches the
darkness. Each tear that falls, we are
happy to know there is HOPE.*

*We offer our services to spiritual life
willingly - to learn - to understand and
then to pass on the light which is HOPE!*

CHAPTER 1

INTRODUCTION

This book is meant to be used as a tool to help you begin your journey of understanding and to help you communicate with your ancestors and spirit guides/eguns, which is accomplished through prayers, divination, rituals, and offerings. The act of communicating with spirits falls under the domain of spiritualism. Although the practice and essence of spiritualism is ancient, since 1983 the US Government has recognized it as a religion. "Spiritualism is defined as a scientific, philosophical, and religious practice that proves the continuity of life after death through demonstrated communication between mediums/ spiritualists and those who reside in the spirit world."[1] Spiritualism is a science because it uses observation and research to describe and explain spiritual phenomena through mediumship. *Science* simply means knowledge that is attained through study and practice. Therefore, through the practice of mediumship, the spirit world is explored for various truths about human and spirit life. In Latin communities, these truths are called *evidencias*, or evidence, and the practice of spiritualism is called *Espiritismo*; a Spanish word used to describe the combined mediumistic practices begun by French spiritist, Allan Kardec. Spiritual information is interpreted and given by mediums to be used as verification and support from the realm of spirit.

Spiritualism also supports philosophical views and questions about how people should live (ethics and morals), what sorts of things exist, and metaphysics as it relates to the ultimate nature of being and the world. Although spiritualism is incorporated into and is the base of many spiritual/religious systems, it can absolutely stand on its own, with no limitations regarding the levels that are accessible for connecting with God/nature and the various levels of spirit beings. The only limitations are human limitations. Many view "spiritualism as a common sense religion, meaning that it accepts all truths found within the universe, nature, other spiritual and religious systems, literature, science, and the divine and natural laws," per www.nsac.org.

The bottom line is this: true spiritualism is about gaining and accepting truth as it exists within the universe. Truth or trust is one of the most basic and fundamental laws of nature and the universe. Accepting truth, whether in your day-to-day or spiritual life, requires one to have courage, no matter what, in the face of fear, illusion, lies and deception. Now, the information in *this* book is in its general form, because the first truth is that within our own cultures, we each have our own way of doing things. And the second truth is that I am merely sharing knowledge that I have acquired during my own personal journey towards the contentment of my soul.

I hope you will find the following information enlightening; my wish is for you to understand the complexity of ancestor and spirit veneration through simple and easy-to-understand explanations. My experiences, both good and bad, prompted me to write this book. Many of you may agree with what I say, some may not, and some may even be offended, which is not my intention. My only intention is to inform interested devotees of both sides of the coin. This is where my story begins.

Over the years, I have faced many trials and tribulations in trying to cross over from my old life into the new. As an Afrikan-Amerikan female brought up in a predominantly Hispanic neighborhood, with many Hispanic friends, in many ways I had always been exposed to the philosophy of the spiritual system or religion called Lukumi/Yoruba. When I was younger, I knew this system as Santeria. When I went to the homes of my friends, their parents had altars with statues, pictures, and glasses of water placed upon them. In retrospect, I never really questioned what I saw; I just thought it was a part of the décor Spanish people had because of their culture. I was oblivious to the whole thing—to the underlying philosophy of what was going on. Now that I think about it, being as young as I was and being brought up in church, I never really paid attention to any of the cultures outside of my Baptist upbringing, but as I grew up and became more independent, things changed—life changed. In my late teens, I noticed that my surroundings seemed different: people were different, and what was, was no longer. I was realizing that everyone was getting older—I was getting older—and we all had newfound responsibilities and different roads to follow. I found myself facing many harsh dilemmas; while doing this, I knew that I needed something, but I didn't know quite what it was.

I had a pretty healthy and stable childhood, and by eighteen I had a daughter and had graduated from high school. I lived with my daughter's father for a while but eventually left him because of his abuse, at which point I went to live with my girlfriend's mom. The situation was ideal for both of us because I needed a babysitter in the daytime and my friend's mom needed a babysitter at night, so between the two of us things worked out really well. By this time, I was in trade school and had my own money. My life was pretty good for a person my age, and by twenty, my mom moved and gave me her five-room apartment, which was more than enough space for my daughter and me.

I was the type of individual who always wanted to excel, and for the most part, I always kept a positive attitude. As a matter of fact, most people called me Smiley, because every time they saw me I had a smile on my face, although on many occasions I was not smiling inside. But no matter what, I always maintained a positive attitude and I felt that there was nothing that I could not do. I could be whatever I wanted to be, even with a baby, so I focused on excelling, and I did.

I found out that many people in the neighborhood were jealous; they didn't understand how I was able to do and get the things I wanted. I figured, "Hello! It's called working." I remember thinking, "People are stupid. Why would someone be jealous about another person trying to do something good for themselves?" People really began to confuse me, and I remember feeling different or foreign and that I did not fit in. I guess I assumed that everyone thought the same way I did in terms of wanting to excel and have the finer things in life, but lo and behold, I quickly learned the meaning of the phrase "misery loves company."

At this point, I had been on my own for about two years. I took care of my daughter the best I could, and luckily for me I had enough family support so that I didn't have to worry about her at all. My daughter's grandmother (on her father's side) had my daughter spoiled rotten, and she would literally pick my daughter up every weekend, or I would drop her off to spend the weekend. This gave me a break and peace of mind. However, slowly but progressively, over about a year, things in my life began to go downhill until I hit what felt like the bottom of the pit. I was depressed and confused. I had a good job making decent money, but the money never seemed to stay in my hands. I continued to feel as if I would go one step forward and three backward. Literally, my world felt as if it was turned upside down. More and more I began to feel a huge void in my life. I began feeling emptier and emptier by the day. I would go home, and when the opportunity presented itself I would just sleep; that was my hideaway. I guess I was hoping to wake up to a better day, but somehow my decent life had turned into a kind of hell. I remember feeling lost and out of control. This was very unusual for me—I was someone who was never out of control. I did not quite know how to handle my unfortunate life. Things had gotten so bad that I remember having suicidal thoughts on one particular day. Thankfully, I was able to push these thoughts out of my mind as quickly as they had entered. That was not me. However, I did feel as if I were going crazy. How could this be? I always had my head together. Were things so bad that I actually felt that I would lose control? I knew that everyone had their own cross to bear, but jeez! I began thinking that God was punishing me. I knew I was not a bad person; I was the type of person who would give away what I had if somebody else needed it. If they needed help, I would help them. I respected people. I stayed out of trouble. I've always been a believer of the Golden Rule: Do unto others as you would have them do unto you!

At first I wondered if there was something wrong with me, but when I analyzed myself, I knew that there wasn't. I was good-looking, intelligent, well-balanced, independent, well-groomed, and nicely dressed. Nah, there was nothing wrong with me! Then I started to wonder if something was wrong within my apartment. I didn't know it then, but the energy was off. I felt that maybe my apartment was bad luck. The air felt very heavy. When I was home, I would continually feel drained to the point where I would constantly fall asleep. I would have sporadic good days, but they were short lived. My boyfriends were decent guys with jobs and goals, but they, too, would only stay temporarily. At one point, I was so depressed that my house turned into the party house, the hangout spot, but in the end I knew that was not me, either—that lifestyle just was not for me. I guess I needed something to make me feel alive and to pass the time, something to bring me happiness, because I didn't know what the hell was going on or what I was going to do. I began to discover that the friends I had for so long were not really my friends. Every time I turned around, they were putting me in some "he said, she said" drama.

My life was becoming so freakin' chaotic that I just couldn't take it anymore. It was the same grind, day in and day out, until one day, while sitting on my bed, some weird thoughts entered my mind. It was like there was another voice in my head and it was telling me that the negativity and evil that surrounded me didn't belong to me and what was happening to me was not a part of God's plan. I don't remember everything specifically, but it seemed as if a light bulb had finally come on. I remember the voice saying, "This is not your life; this is a life that someone wants for you." Although I didn't quite understand and it took me time to process it, I knew that this voice had to be saying the truth. At that time, I didn't know that I was hearing my spirit guides answering my questions regarding what was wrong with my life, but it made perfect sense to me that this voice had to be right. Feeling confident that I had figured out an important aspect of my problem, I now needed a solution. I was at a point where I knew I had to make changes— quickly. So I did the only thing I knew how to do. I isolated myself—moderately—from everyone and everything I felt was not any good for me, and I focused on myself, turned to prayer, and asked God to show me the way.

Over a period of weeks, and then months, I consistently prayed every morning and every night. During this time, I had three dreams of burning a white candle. I had no clue what it meant, for I knew nothing of candle burning or its mystical effects. (It was naïve of me, but I thought that candles were only burned when the utility company turned out the lights in your home.) The dreams immediately caught my attention, and because I had asked God to show me what was wrong with my life and how to change it, I knew there was no way he would steer me wrong. I felt compelled to follow and investigate. I also felt that God had given me a sign and that this would be the beginning of something that would change my life forever.

Desperate to better my life, and with curiosity leading the way, I learned more and more about candle burning and its association to spirit by talking to as many people as I could. At first, because of what I was taught in church and what I was sure people would think, I felt as if I was doing something bad or evil. I began questioning my religious beliefs and myself. What side of the fence was I on—good or evil? To gain some level of comfort, I would go to this Catholic Church near 35th Street in Manhattan to pray at the feet of the Sacred Heart of Jesus statue. I prayed for weeks asking Jesus to help me and give me a sign if what I was doing was evil. I told Jesus that I was confused and that I kept having these dreams showing me unfamiliar spirit things and that I didn't want to do anything that was/is associated with evil. The more I prayed to Jesus, the more dreams I would have. So I assumed that working with candles was okay. And as time went on, I began to feel better but a part of me still wasn't sure. Even so, I instinctively felt as if something was pushing me to follow the dreams I'd been having. As I followed the guidance of my dreams, things became clearer and clearer, confirming every day that I was indeed doing the right thing, and all the while, it felt so natural. That is when I realized that God had turned me on to something that was exciting, mystical, and powerful all at the same time. After burning one white candle a week for three weeks, I went to a huge botanica store on Webster Avenue in the Bronx. It was an overwhelming experience. The store had thousands of products: anointing oils, books, candles, herbs, powders, sacred images, and on and on. I felt like I was in a huge candy store: I wanted to buy it all. Out of all the products I could have purchased, I bought a candle with an image of an Amerikan Indian on it. For some reason, I was just attracted to it. At that time, I didn't know that the Native Amerikan Indian was one of my guardian spirits, helping me all the time. This was it for me. The information I received about—and from—the products became an addiction. I spent many hours at the store, looking around and buying books, trying to absorb as much information as I could.

A book that interested me immediately was *Voodoo and Hoodoo: The Craft as Revealed by Traditional Practitioners* by Jim Haskins. I purchased it because it had a section about laying a trick for ill will, which is using a spell or witchcraft to cause harm. I couldn't believe that people would actually give instructions on how to harm someone else. I was amazed and naïve about the whole premise that people actually used witchcraft to cause other people harm, to dominate or control them, or to win a court case, even. For the life of me, I will never understand why someone would want to hurt another individual through supernatural means, but after reading this book as well as many others, I was convinced that I was a victim of foul play. I decided that I needed to learn everything I possibly could, good and bad, about the motives that drive people to such lengths, but I also needed a strategy to combat the ill will—the

8

witchcraft—that was ruining my life.

This inspired me to continue burning the white candle and the Indian candle, for I was comfortable with just those two. Strangely enough, I started to notice things as they burned. The candle glass would be totally black when the candle finished, or the candles would burst or crack, which made me extremely scared and curious at the same time. It was weird, but I had some sort of feeling that it meant something, and I wanted to know more, so I began to research and asked a lot of questions. Back then, in the late 80's, it was not easy getting answers. I didn't realize that such information was kept so secret, and the fact that people were evasive only made me want to forge ahead and delve deeper into this mystery.

Ironically, even with all the obstacles I encountered while trying to get answers to my questions in reference to candle burning, I discovered that people are placed in your path for a reason and that God makes a way for you to get what you need when you need it most. I say this because I needed information and God put two elderly Hispanic women in my path. These woman were called in to help on my job with a special mailing and being that they were there for a couple of days, I decided to ask them if they knew what it meant when a candle glass turns black or when the candle glass breaks. Luckily for me, one of the women worked in a botanica store that sold religious/spiritual products. She briefly explained that candles are physical representations of our prayers and it is believed that as the flame burns, it repeats our prayers many times over. Burning candles with prayers and intention in a candle spell provides light and energy to the spirit world. And in response, our spirit guides have a way of using the energy from candles to communicate back to us in a way that we can effectively interpret. For instance, when my candle glass turned totally black, such as what I encountered with the Indian candle—

my first botanica purchase—and my white candle, this meant that some sort of negativity or witchcraft was affecting me. The women also explained that when a candle cracked and/or burst, this meant that my spirit guides used the candle to absorb or block an intense amount of negativity or evil that was trying to hurt or attack me. From that day on I was hooked, and the road opened to me in miraculous ways.

Approximately four months later, while going to work one day, I saw a palm reader's sign on one of the side streets at 40th Street and Lexington Avenue in Manhattan and decided to go the next step. "What could it hurt?" I thought. My memories are vague, but the palm reader told me that I would live a long life. She told me about the men in my life. And, among other things, she said that I was meant to be somebody in this world. Cautiously, I wondered if she told everybody the same stuff just for the money, but then she proceeded to tell me about the negativity that was hindering me in my life, and I perked up. My eyes opened wider. I was still a little skeptical about her authenticity, but I was so curious that I went along with the reading anyway, because I needed help. Initially, I think her motives were purely monetary, but then our relationship changed over a three-month period. She became more concerned. I saw her maybe six times, and she started to see the evil that surrounded me in my home. Unfamiliar with the process of what she could do for me, I still wasn't sure if I should believe her, but she started to hit on things that she couldn't have known. I decided to go ahead and trust her, but only to a limit. As a remedy, this palm reader gave me things to put in a shoebox for protection, and she gave me blessed candles and incense to burn in my home on a daily basis. I really cannot vouch for the shoebox ritual, but when I burned the frankincense, I immediately noticed a difference. The air felt lighter and breezier, and there was a peace that I had never before felt in my home. Even my friends noticed it; I remember a close friend of mine sitting on my floor and commenting about how peaceful my home felt. This was reassuring, because there was someone validating what I originally felt after burning the incense. After some time, I realized that this palm reader was my first stepping-stone towards something bigger (spiritually speaking), but our relationship ended when she told me that she could no longer help me because the energy that I was fighting was too strong for her to handle. As a result, I became very discouraged that I was on my own once again.

A little while later, one hot summer day, I was sitting outside in front of my building, feeling sad and depressed. I was doing poorly at that time. I didn't even have money to get to work. This was when I truly saw who my friends were, because there were a few people who owed me money; one of them had the money but refused to repay me. It really bothered me because I was in dire need financially, and it felt bad that my so-called friends were not there for me in the way that I had been there for them. Then a neighbor whom I had never spoken to approached me, and we started talking. As the weeks went by, we talked more and more. I explained what I was going through and that I needed some serious help. I didn't realize at that time that the help I needed was of a spiritual nature, though it was. We became friends, and she soon introduced me to her godmother, a spiritualist, known as an *espiritista* (can be a male or female) in the Latin community. This woman was incredible and truly made me a believer in the practice of spiritualism. I was mesmerized by how the spiritual work she did actually came to fruition.

She did not take to me right away. I remember her saying that she did not know if she wanted to take on any additional godchildren, but as time went on she kept working with me. Eventually, I was familiar with séance, communing, praying, rituals, working with spirits, and how to use the tools of the trade—candles, oils, powders, herbs, baths, and floor washes. I caught on quickly and learned more and more; I was a natural. After about a year or so, she moved to Florida. I thought, "Here I go on my own, once again." However, I moved forward. Although I bounced around for a while looking for a spiritual home, now, twenty-plus years after I started burning candles, I am a priestess of Lukumi/Yoruba and Palo Mayombe within the Afrikan diaspora. And believe me, it was a long, hard road, mainly because of the pain, suffering, and sacrifices I faced along the way, many occurring because of the negative and evil thoughts and actions of other people.

Amongst my many hard lessons, I quickly learned that people's hearts were not as clean as mine. I encountered many so-called spiritualists, priests, and priestesses who were very selfish and insecure, many wanting nothing more than power, control, and money. They had no desire to teach what was right. This is sad; they give the good spiritualists, priests, and priestesses a bad name. When seekers are learning, they are not sure what is right and what is wrong, but at least God gave them common sense and intuition; they just need to learn how to use and trust it. For lack of discernment, I was misled in so many ways, but I thank God that I had built a spiritual relationship with my spirit guides early in the game, because they were the ones who helped me out of many traps.

As hard as it may be to understand, I am thankful for my hardships and bad experiences: experience is the best teacher in the world. Those experiences were also my tests (the path of being a true shaman is to be stripped down and spiritually rebuilt), to prove that I can make it past all the obstacles that have been and will be placed in my path as I journey onward. I know that having made it through them is what makes me a strong individual and helps build my character. I also know that those experiences are preparing me for the future. Because of what I went through, I am now able to pave a smoother road for those who follow. And I know that this road is not for everyone; however, if a person decides to choose this path, his or her destiny, ancestors, and spirit guides will, in some way, form, or fashion, give them the necessary indications. I have determined that my goal will involve promoting higher evolution for spirit and humankind and properly teaching and guiding all those who truly aspire to learn the philosophy of spiritualism.

My journey has been long, but I have remained open to the teachings of the spirits. I haven't always understood, but things have worked out for me thus far. And as I begin to share what I have learned, individuals are starting to seek me out. I am not quite sure how to handle this, only because it is difficult for me to feel that I have enough training and knowledge to work with other people and their circumstances. However, now that I am a priestess, I am determined to be the best that I can be and I have decided to give this work my all with the highest of integrity – I would not have it any other way. If I could not do that, I would not feel worthy of priesthood. Through it all, I remain hopeful and positive. I will not let the dogma of the world get me down or change my outlook on this very beautiful form of spiritualism and the religion of Lukumi.

I know that what sets me apart from my counterparts is my quest for growth, knowledge, and righteousness. I have a destiny to fulfill and God has placed me in this world, assisted by my spirit guides/eguns and Òrìsà, to save lost souls and lives. Because there are a lot of charlatans, I will be there to make things right to the best of my abilities, especially for those who have become victims of bad spiritual circumstances. The spirit guides have taught me that my growth can be infinite, the gifts can be bountiful, and anything is possible through FAITH and

DETERMINATION.

The best feelings in the world come from the relationships that I have developed with my guardian spirits. I have had so many exciting, beautiful, powerful, and even frightening experiences with the spirits. But I know that they love me unconditionally. Who could ask for more? They have helped me love and understand people better, and they are teaching me to be non-judgmental because of the simple fact that no one is perfect. Of course, these lessons are a part of everyday life processes, but I cannot envision my life without them. The spirits are my extended family and I love them dearly, and I am glad to know that I am on the right path. This philosophy of ancestor and Òrìsà veneration can be very complex and confusing, especially if taught wrong. So I thank all of the people who have helped me along the way. I thank them for their knowledge and contributions, no matter how seemingly small, and I thank all my guides for giving me this opportunity and this book as a way to reach out and share with the world.

For all of you interested in this journey, respect God, your ancestors, and your family—whether biological or spiritual—and blessings will come. It will not always be peaches and cream; despite the bad press, the negativity, and the hardships, we must continue to strive for evolution through service to spirit and our human companions; however, I hope that this book gives you a positive outlook on a powerful spiritual practice that was saved—against many odds and by many ethnic groups. As an Afrikan-Amerikan woman, I want to thank those groups, for without them, we all would have missed out on a very important part of our heritage, particularly here in the West.

Health or sickness; wealth or poverty; success or failure – all begin in the mind. Your physical body and material affairs reflect your state of mind. The person with a positive attitude and a strong belief in health prevents sickness from entering his life.

–Rev. Ike

WORDS OF WISDOM

Not only did the Afrikans suffer religious and spiritual persecution, so, too, did millions of Native Amerikan tribes. They suffered physical, sexual, and emotional abuse from European Catholic missionaries, and as a means for survival, many converted to Catholicism. These missionaries deemed Native Amerikan spirituality worthless and a superstition inspired by Satan, who we know as the Christian devil.

Native Amerikan cosmology differs from tribe to tribe, as does Afrikan cosmology, but for most, there is a general belief that there is one God and all life is sacred. Native Amerikan prayer does not consist of attending church, using a bible, or kneeling with praying hands. Native Amerikans commune with the Great Spirit by smoking a ceremonial pipe; they attend sweat lodges instead of church; and they sit as the essence of sweet grass sweeps their bodies in order to spiritually cleanse, while the smoke carries their prayers to the heavens. Furthermore, Native Amerikans believe that the medicine wheel represents the journey each individual must take to find their own path:

> Let us lend our ways and learn the ways of others for the greater good of world harmony. Let us respect the earth in which we live and respect our brothers and sisters no matter how different.
>
> Let us always do what is right in truth and take responsibility for our actions, and let the wisdom of our ancestors teach us the lessons hidden in life.
>
> And finally, let us remain close to the Great Spirit, our creator, to be free to find and follow our own path and the spirituality of our ancestors.

—Words of Wisdom by Oba Ilari Aladokun, inspired by my Native Amerikan Ancestors

THE GREAT INDIAN SPIRIT PRAYER
By Oba Ilari Aladokun

Great Warrior Spirit, my watcher, I offer you words of reverence. I am calling upon you, and I am seeking your assistance from the toil of the living world. Therefore, my great spirit, I need your guidance and protection along the way—every day. Provide me with the necessary tools and resources to survive in this world, and give my family and me your blessings of luck, health, and prosperity.

Protect me from the treacheries, pitfalls, and traps of my adversaries, and let your poisonous arrows kill the negative thought forms and evil intentions of my enemies. I have faith in your power, I have faith in your courage, and I have faith in your strength. Teach me to develop these same attributes so that I can gain the force necessary to remove all obstacles from my path.

Great Spirit and mother earth, I come unto you, pure in thoughts, with clean hands and a clean heart. I need your ancient wisdom so that I can learn to respect and appreciate the gifts that have been given to me. And as you teach and prepare me for your lessons, may I learn them well, for my mind is open to absorb your great knowledge and wisdom.

And in conclusion, my great Indian spirit, I give thanks for your love and protection and for all that you do even when I am not aware. I thank you always, and I ask that you continually bless me. I will pray the same for you. As so it was spoken, let it be!

AHO MITAKUYE OYASIN PRAYER

"The phrase translates as "all my relatives," "we are all related," or "all my relations." It is a prayer of oneness and harmony with all forms of life: other people, animals, birds, insects, trees and plants, and even rocks, rivers, mountains and valleys.

Aho Mitakuye Oyasin - All my relations. I honor you in this circle of life with me today. I am grateful for this opportunity to acknowledge you in this prayer.

- *To the Creator, for the ultimate gift of life, I thank you.*
- *To the mineral nation that has built and maintained my bones and all foundations of life experience, I thank you.*
- *To the plant nation that sustains my organs and body and gives me healing herbs for sickness, I thank you.*
- *To the animal nation that feeds me from your own flesh and offers your loyal companionship in this walk of life, I thank you.*
- *To the human nation that shares my path as a soul upon the sacred wheel of Earthly life, I thank you.*
- *To the Spirit nation that guides me invisibly through the ups and downs of life and for carrying the torch of light through the Ages, I thank you. To the Four Winds of Change and Growth, I thank you.*
- *You are all my relations, my relatives, without whom I would not live. We are in the circle of life together, co-existing, co-dependent, co-creating our destiny. One, not more important than the other. One nation evolving from the other and yet each dependent upon the one above and the one below. All of us a part of the Great Mystery. Great Spirit, thank you for this life."*[xi]

CHAPTER 2

CALLING OF THE SPIRIT

Many of you were raised in some congregation and indoctrinated with Christian beliefs (whether Baptist, Methodist, A.M.E., Lutheran, Pentecostal, Catholic, or something else) and now have grown to adulthood, somehow feeling there is something else calling to your spirit. Moreover, you sense that what is calling to your spirit is outside of all the conveniences and comforts that modern day society has awarded you. And even with the freedom that science and technology has provided, as a member of society you are increasingly unhappy, increasingly unsatisfied, and even more unfulfilled than your predecessors could imagine.

A feeling of incompleteness and an emptiness that at one time or another you thought you could satisfy and escape by using alcohol or drugs or by obtaining wealth, sex, power, marriage, family, or love from some other individual troubles many of you. Then, as each day progresses into another, you realize that you live in a perverted society that is plagued with famine, disease, crime, and illness. The family structure is breaking down, communities are breaking down, and even the earth is breaking down.

Though people surround you, you feel lost, confused, and alone. You reach out, but you see nothing, you feel nothing. You search for answers, for solutions—but nothing. No one can help, and you try everything physical and material within your power, but the void is still there. Even with all of this, you continue to feel that something is calling to your spirit, sending you on a path-finding journey to fulfillment.

To answer the call of the *spirit*, the inner guide, many people are broadening their beliefs and education regarding spiritual/religious systems from around the world. And many do not understand or realize that it is the *soul*, their very own *soul* that is searching for *the* spiritual home that will bring it peace. This is becoming particularly true for Black Amerikans[2] who were primarily raised within Christian doctrines of various denominations. Those of you from this background know that many Christians are ignorant of any belief outside of the Bible or Jesus Christ. For example, the following is an actual statement e-mailed to me by a closed-minded Christian believer:

> *"God of the Bible forbids the worship of anything or anyone except Himself, as idolatry. And Jesus says in Luke 16:26 that there is a great chasm (a wall that cannot be crossed) placed between the dead and the living, and that they cannot communicate with us, nor can we communicate with them. They also proclaim that the Bible teaches that those spiritual beings who claim to be 'spirit guides,' are actually masquerading demons of deception and are sent to ensnare us into Satan's kingdom, by diverting us from believing in the Salvation and Eternal Life that is made available to us only through belief in Jesus Christ."*

My response to this individual was:

> *"There is nothing devilish or masqueraded in the advice that I*

have received from my ancestors and spirit guides. For me and for millions of others, spirit communication has proven the continuity of life after death. I am a priestess initiated into the ways of the Afrikan ancestors, and they have brought nothing but goodness into my life, and because of such, no 'Bible' or man-made doctrine written by man can tell me otherwise. The proof is in my life—it has flourished. I have nothing but good and loving people in my home, on my job, and an excellent support system, etc. I treat people the way I expect to be treated (the golden rule), and I live everyday to do nothing but good deeds, and because of that, I am blessed. My experience through ancestor worship has been wonderful and has healed many lives. What is masqueraded is all the "so-called Christians" who pretend to be Holy, saved, and love Jesus and live devilish lives everyday— many of them sitting directly in the congregation shouting hallelujah or standing directly up on the pulpit committing every sin underneath the sun. Not all are this way, just as not all who have been called toward a different path, a non-Christian path, are devilish."

My intentions are not to dispute Christian beliefs but to simply broaden the scope of spiritual and religious phenomena beyond Christian ideology. When I read the statement in the e-mail message it disappointed me, because when I open my mind, look at the world, and listen to world history, common sense tells me that the statement is not solely true. Is Christianity powerful? Heck yeah! However, when I look at the word idolatry, I say to myself, "What are the Christians really saying?" *The New Webster's Comprehensive Dictionary* defines idolatry as blind adoration; it also states that an idol can be a statue, a symbol, a god, a deity—one that is blindly adored. Now, if it's true that no one should idolize anything or anyone except for Jesus himself, then why do devout Catholics have blind adoration for the many statues they have standing in their churches all around the world, such as the Virgin Mary and various angels and saints for whom candles and incense are lit and burned on a daily basis?

I have no problem with this, except when someone tells me that because my "idols" are not associated with or look like the perceived image of Jesus, then I have joined the ranks of Satan. Are we to believe that there is just one face and one representative of God? Maybe on an individual level, but if we expand our minds to look at the world as a whole and include all the spiritual systems that inspire love, forgiveness, peace, or wholeness through healing, there would be no doubt that God, as the Creator of all, has many names, faces, and disciples, with Jesus being just one of them. All of these names, faces, and disciples have specific paths and purposes of assisting the living to fulfill their soul's destiny.

It would make sense that the essences of God would have been distributed around the world, because no two people resonate or gravitate toward all of the same things all of the time. In this way, God has the opportunity to assist and save as many individuals and souls as possible through the implementation of many different religious and spiritual systems versus trying to make everyone adhere to just one holy disciple.

In the case of Jesus, one of God's leading authorities on earth was a man born with a purpose and a path to follow — a path that led to persecution because his beliefs were different, as was the case for many holy disciples and deities. And for as much respect as I have for Jesus, I know that he has just as much respect and love for me because I have followed my path — a path that was determined by my soul and the Creator before my birth. It is funny, because I used to be one of those Christians who only knew about the Bible and Jesus, and back then I considered myself content with my Christian guidance and beliefs. Although I was not searching for any kind of spiritual awareness, a twist of fate and a series of events led me down the path of becoming an initiated, practicing priestess of ancestor and Òrìsà/nature veneration, Lukumi/ Yoruba.

Most Christians would undoubtedly say that I am practicing sorcery, witchcraft, or devil work, and my soul is damned to hell, for this was and still is the New World slave-indoctrinating notion that anything and everything out of Afrika is bad, ugly, and evil— including the people, their cultures, and their beliefs. Sadly, yet understandably, our ancestors have passed these awful notions from generation to generation. We just cannot get the thought out of our heads that Black is somehow not beautiful, even though Black is truly and profoundly beautiful.

What about all of our Native Amerikan, Afrikan, and Asian ancestors who practiced their traditions thousands and thousands of years prior to *Christ*? Are their souls condemned to the eternal fire? Does God believe that individuals are ugly and evil because of their skin color? And what about all the other religious groups and cultures from around the world, such as Egypt, China, Japan, Melanesia, and India (including the Native Amerikans, Afrikans, and Asians) who continue to practice beliefs different from the *Christ* conscious concept? Will God, as the Creator of all, love or help them any less? I don't think so! And it is arrogant and racist to believe this.

In addition to our religious upbringing, since childhood we have been inundated with positive and/or negative programming from our parents and society, leaving us with a whole bunch of rules and regulations, dos and don'ts, prejudices, insecurities, dogmas, and fears. For some of us, we were lucky if we ended up with love, security, and happiness, or any combination thereof. But as we grew up trying to sort through all the programs, we forgot who we are. The world has taught us to become prisoners of mind control, racism, sexism, materialism, and financial gain instead of seeking spiritual refuge. Doesn't our currency say, "In God We Trust"?

Value is no longer placed on the bare essentials of food, shelter, clothing, and health. For some, the Creator is only thought of when times are bad or when there is some state of crisis, tragedy, or misfortune. It is during hard times that people try to evaluate and regain their relationship and trust with God and spirit. They have placed undue value on how much they can acquire materialistically and financially, even though many have no clue about the means to obtain those things. No longer do they fight for freedom, education, healthcare, or justice as a priority in the way the elders once did. In the eyes of most, "The Almighty Dollar" has become "God." The more they have, the more they want. We live in a society of "Give me now! I want now!" and the greed is never satisfied. Many have set their sights on the possessions of the world, and in return, we are all losing the battles of freedom, education, healthcare, and justice.

We need to be reminded that materialism and financial gains, in most cases, provide temporary satisfaction—these things cannot really make us happy, and often lead us to become prisoners of debt, whether financially, mentally, emotionally, or physically. Basically, God has been forgotten, and the sacred purpose for human existence continues to be muddled. We have been put to sleep and led astray, and all the while our souls are calling to us, trying to awaken us to be led back to our true selves before it is too late.

For those of you who are beginning to awaken—or maybe you are already there—you are probably consciously or subconsciously beginning to rebel on the soul level and go against the dogma, programs and the beliefs that have been taught to you, just to satisfy that calling. Many people are now realizing that they have to set their sights and hearts on the divine and rely on the inner and outer spirit worlds for the satisfaction and peace they seek. Know that deviating from your original upbringing will be met with opposition, controversy, skepticism, and attempts to make you feel guilty, but only awareness of self will bring peace and stability into your life. And of course, you will need to follow a system that is going to satisfy your inner calling. Know thyself and to thyself be true. This statement truly sums it all up. There is no accident in the spiritual path you (the soul) have chosen before coming to this world; we all have chosen our destinies and paths before birth. Your challenge and purpose are to fulfill your destiny during this life or the next.

To me, God has no specific religion or creed; we are just facilitators of God's universal energy—both negative and positive. Maybe you are supposed to learn specific lessons of the virtues and inequities of a spiritual system outside the one in which you were raised to increase your greatness in God's eyes. Knowledge is power and experience is the true teacher; therefore, all that is positive and negative within the universe will teach us more about our Creator and ourselves, and how to do a better job of spiritually preparing our families and communities.

I believe that I have the best of all worlds. I believe in God, first and foremost; I believe in the Gospel according to Christ because this was my foundation and upbringing; I trust in my ancestors, spirit guides/teachers; and I trust in the Òrìsà. Believing in them is believing in their traditions. It does not mean that I have to practice all these beliefs; it just means that my mind is open to their systems. Besides that, I have Afrikan ancestors, Native Amerikan ancestors, Irish ancestors, Christian ancestors, and a host of others that I do not even know, but to the best of my abilities I pay homage to them all. Nonetheless, all of these spirit energies make up a part of who I am (living in my DNA), as do their beliefs.

And as with many faiths, we all want to have a close relationship with the Creator; therefore, I am blessed to have opened my mind enough to encompass all the different facets of my Creator.

In actuality, I feel enriched with blessings from my international lineage, and I do not think that God minds one bit because he knows that he has truly contributed to my greatness, and for this I give praise. So who can argue that I have chosen the wrong path or say that I am damned to hell for practicing and believing in something outside Christian theology, damned especially by those who do not understand or who think it is insane to have knowledge of more than one system? Not even the most religious person in the world can say that they know the true intentions of the Creator. Even today, while there are so many people searching outside their familiar territory for their calling, venturing onto foreign ground, I do believe that you need one main system as your guide and foundation, but having additional knowledge and education about other spiritual systems can be, if nothing else, informative. We only fear what we do not know or understand; therefore, I know that if we have knowledge of other religions and spiritual systems, we can learn to respect other people and their beliefs without judgments or fear.

"We are a rainbow culture, and like the rainbow each color is different and has its own energy and properties. One color alone is just that, alone, but when a single color lends its properties and overlaps into the next color, it has assisted in the makeup of something so beautiful—a complete rainbow."

by Oba Ilari Aladokun

CHAPTER 3

DRUMMING OF THE BEAT

I have been placed on a road that follows the drumming beat of my ancestors; "where is this road taking me?" Where will I end up? It's like following footprints in the dark. I don't know where I'm going, but the beat is what calls to my spirit—my soul—so I follow. This time, I will not find myself at a dead end, as was destined for them (my ancestors)! I am a slave to no one—to no one thing. They say, "Follow me; follow the beat where you will find freedom—freedom of faith and freedom of your soul." This following has led me to the ways of the old—reverence of nature and the ancestors—ways that I will try to share for your greater understanding.

The practice of nature veneration and ancestor reverence (worship) amongst Afrikans constitutes a tradition called Yoruba or Ifa, considered to be the "Father" of all religions and is thousands and thousands of years old. During the slave trade and the Middle Passage, millions of Afrikans of various ethnicities were transported to so-called New World countries like Brazil, Cuba, Haiti, Jamaica, and Puerto Rico, as well as the United States. After being stripped, robbed, and raped of their heritage, the slaves became inundated with New World views and new ways of life. Out of fear, many of them decided to submit to these new ways as a means of survival, whereas other enslaved Afrikans, just as fearful for their lives, fought and modified their practices by using Christianity as the mask to hide and maintain their traditional beliefs in order to save whatever principles they had left. During this move from the lands of Afrika, a very important aspect of communication was stripped away; the use of drums was banned in order to keep the slaves from sending secret messages. The slaveholders feared that the Afrikans would organize an uprising. But surprisingly, the enslaved people were still able to creatively kill two birds with one stone by cleverly orchestrating special meetings using the denseness of the woods or by pretending to have prayer circles and church services in different locations. In this way they kept the "masta" in the dark, allowing themselves to discreetly and safely practice their traditions in hiding.

"While attending these special meetings, they were also able to create hand signals and encoded songs with secret messages, which allowed them the ability to maintain devotion and receive spirit messages through preaching and laying on of hands to heal and receive various forms of spirit possession, which involved shouting, dancing, or speaking in foreign languages, known as speaking in tongues. In the New World, many view this as a manifestation of receiving the Holy Ghost. Even with every attempt made to keep the enslaved people from continuing with their Afrikan spirituality, rituals, and traditions, the concept of nature, spirit, and ancestor veneration has not only survived, but it has been embraced on a global scale."[3]

Many consider Afrika to be the mother who gave birth to all life. But from a religious standpoint, and as with many other cultures, our Afrikan ancestors believed in only *one* God who created all and is the ultimate overseer of society.

"This supreme god was, and still is, considered to have the final say in all matters, is the guardian of moral code, and is the judge and jury who punishes evildoers and rewards the righteous. Along with God, the ancestors, too, are considered guardians of morality; they give approval of actions that are in the best interest of family and the community and disapprove of actions that are harmful and disruptive to their adherents. In Afrika, people believe that the ancestors can sentence individuals, as well as communities, to punishments of disease, illness, impotence, misfortune, poverty, tragedy, and death. They may also reward those who adhere to the moral laws of family and community with children, fertility, good harvest, good health, long life, peace, and prosperity. The ancestors are believed to act as the invisible policemen, enforcing the moral laws of their community."[x]

What is an ancestor? Who can be considered an ancestor? Depending on the culture, the definition of ancestor has many meanings. In some cultures, you cannot be considered an ancestor unless you have lived a good-standing, morally correct life; that is, a life without immorality or criminal harm to others. In other cultures, women are not considered ancestors at all. However, for most (and generally speaking), ancestor veneration or reverence, which means maintaining an ongoing relationship with those who have physically departed (died), is not only a tradition shared amongst our Afrikan ancestors, but also a concept that has existed through almost every known culture, including various parts of Afrika, the Pacific, certain parts of India and Indochina, and Indonesia, and also among those who have converted to Islam or Christianity. Even Jewish people have been known to light candles and say special prayers honoring a family member's anniversary of death. And in celebration of All Soul's Day, many honor the dead by putting gifts, flowers, and food on the graves of their family members, for many cultures believe that after death, the physical body is left to decay and the soul transits into the spirit realm, where it continues to live as an ancestor.

Also, in many parts of Afrika, people leave gifts, money, clothes, animals, and messages at the gravesites of deceased relatives, hoping that the deceased might use these items on their journeys. Some cultures also honor the dead with festivals, drumming, singing, dancing, and drinking; they believe that honoring their ancestors is honoring their lineage and roots, which is the first step to reclaiming their spiritual heritage. Therefore, the ancestors are consulted for guidance, prayed to, venerated with rituals, and given offerings for their continued influence on the living by helping them resolve their day-to-day problems.

Because so many cultures, primarily outside of the United States, believe that the invisible world plays such an enormous part in everyday life, it is customary and extremely important to pay a great deal of attention to the dead and the ancestral family. I think we can agree that death is a universal fact and is the inevitable end of all human life. However, in many cultures, the end of physical life does not mean the absolute and complete end of life because the soul continues on, just in another form (invisible) and in another world.

Particularly in Afrika, people believe that the dead are reborn into family members so that they can finish whatever business they were unable to finish while on earth. For this reason, a great deal of concern, care, time, and money is spent on proper burial rites— from the preparation of the body all the way through to the prayers, ceremonies, and sacrifices that are given to help ensure that the deceased is satisfied and appeased for an easy transition from the land of the living to the land of the dead. Many Afrikans feel that if proper funeral rites are not performed for the deceased, the spirit of the dead person will become a ghost who roams the world without peace, lost and confused, but with the abilities to harm and haunt people until it gains the proper attention and burial rights, prayers, offerings, or ceremonies that will bring contentment to its soul.

In Afrika, the ancestors are called egungun; known only as those considered kin (family of the same blood). Egungun was and is a secret society of Yoruba people who believes in the continued existence of ancestors in the lives of the living. They believe that there is a link between the dead and the living and that the egunguns represent ancestral spirits that would return from heaven to visit and periodically commune with the living, especially during a seven-day celebration known as All Soul's Festival, where honor is given and sacrifices are offered at shrines set specifically for the ancestral spirits. During this periodic visit, a chosen member of the egungun society, believed to be possessed by an ancestor, dances through town dressed in native clothing or grass and a wooden mask, accompanied by drummers, while giving spirit messages to the living.

"There are many reasons why the egunguns—ancestor spirits—would come to visit and commune with the living:

- To avert disasters, such as epidemics; to protect the community from harm; and to chase away evil and misfortune that may have befallen the Yoruba society.
- To entertain through drumming, dancing, and magical displays; to encourage social solidarity; and to teach about the laws [of the universe] and customs of their community.
- To enforce moral and behavioral code, punishing or expelling all those who were considered a threat to the well-being of the community, and to help settle

communal disputes.

- To provide medical advice and healing for all those considered ill, whether physically, mentally, emotionally, or spiritually."[x]

In the New World, depending on the culture, the word ancestor has been used interchangeably with the word egun, a shortened form of egungun, which in the New World means spirit of the dead and is used in a broader sense. Therefore, and in general terms, this would mean that eguns would include not only your deceased family members but also all souls and spirit guides who may or may not be related to you.

I choose to use the word ancestor in its traditional form as practiced by my Afrikan predecessors because it is more personal, connective, and empowering, while at the same time emphasizes its true meaning. Also, there are many societies and groups that venerate the ancestors/ egunguns collectively, not just personally, for the community at large. For them, the ancestors/egunguns represent a whole lineage of descendants who are not related but have common goals and purposes that can guide and provide cultural and socioeconomic values to the community as a whole. Furthermore, there are no ceremonies or rituals in this particular religion of Lukumi/Yoruba performed without paying respect to and taking care of the ancestors and spirit guides first, even before the Òrìsà. Here in the Afrikan diaspora, we pay homage to God (Olodumare/Olofi) first, then the ancestors and spirit guides/ eguns so that they can give us their blessings, their protection, and their permission to proceed with our rituals for successful outcomes.

How important is ancestor reverence? Let's see... Try to put yourself in the shoes of your ancestors. If you were an ancestor and your family members were to just forget about you, how would you feel? If you were alone, lost, and confused in the spirit realm, and there was no one praying for you or giving you light so that you could find your way, what would you do? If you wanted to save someone or help them better their life and they just ignored your messages, would you give up? If you wanted forgiveness or just wanted to know that you were still loved, and there was no one to show you some attention or acknowledge your efforts, wouldn't you feel alone and abandoned? And, God forbid, if you were ill and approaching death or you died suddenly, how important would it be to you that someone, even only one person, remembered you? Furthermore, how important would it be that your children remembered you and all of your accomplishments, whether great or not so great?

We live in a society that fears and suppresses death; obviously because no one wants to die, nor do we want our loved ones to die. Because some of us are so uncomfortable with grieving, and the death of loved ones hurts some of us so badly, we try to forget about it altogether. The problem is that many of us focus too much on the negative aspects of death and don't acknowledge the positive. Most of us were taught to mourn and grieve when someone dies. We were rarely taught that we can continue to live with our deceased loved ones for the betterment of our lives.

Our ancestors can help us, advise us, and do things for us from the other side that they could not do when they were alive. They can help us live better, healthier, and more rewarding lives. There is an old saying: out of sight, out of mind. Would you want your loved ones to forget about you just because it is an uncomfortable feeling? Would you want your loved ones to just push you out of their minds when you, as an ancestor, can still serve them well, even on the other side? I don't think any of you would want to be forgotten, because on some level, we all want to be remembered for something. Many of us never think about the fact that we will one day become a spirit, an ancestor; but it is inevitable. And as uncomfortable as it may be, we should think about the legacies that we would like to leave behind. Ask, "How do I want to be remembered?" No matter how you answer this question, remember that your ancestors want to be remembered, too.

The reality of ancestors or spirit guides/eguns is based on faith and conviction. "... When you analyze faith you find that it is a mental attitude against which there is no longer any contradiction in the mind that entertains it. Unfortunately, we find that there is great faith in *fear*. Faith in fear that one may lose his position; faith in fear that one may lose material possessions; faith in the fear that one may lose his health; and so on... Faith is a mental attitude which is so convinced of its own idea—which so completely accepts it—that any contradiction is unthinkable and impossible... Faith is real to the one who experiences it and cannot be denied to the mind of the one who has proven it..."[8] Faith is the confirmation or proof of things not seen, and through this proof we are asking our guardian angels, ancestors, and spirit guides/eguns to intervene and bring us divine blessings. God's infinite power is manifested through our ancestors and guides, so by praying to and honoring them, we petition their guidance to fulfill our divine purpose, become closer with our Creator and to help us become successful and healthy in our everyday lives; at least this is what we should be praying to them for. I must say that spirits are not magicians. We cannot snap our fingers and, presto, have what we want, like genies from a bottle. These are the wrong expectations to have, and you will truly be disappointed if you think this is how it works. The purpose of our ancestors is to help us deal with the good, the bad, and the indifferent, not just hit the lotto. I am not saying that we cannot ask and pray for money or material things, but this should not be the sole reason for praying. *The purpose of prayer is to connect with our ancestors and guides so that they can help us to dodge the negative forces, deal with the contradictions, injustices, and imperfections that exist within life itself.* When we are weak, they help us tap into our strength, and through them we ask that God hears and grants our requests so that we can walk the correct path of our earthly lives towards our destiny.

Conclusively, nature/Òrìsà veneration and ancestor reverence make up a very complex spiritual system, and through this system we receive (Àṣe) the power (the command) and ability to maintain spiritual balance and harmony within the universe, with the ultimate goal of maintaining good character. For the purpose of this book, my primary goal is to focus on the ancestors and spirit guides/eguns that are fundamental parts of our very existence. For general purposes, I refer to eguns as spirit guides, guardian spirits, or spirit protectors and teachers, and ancestors mean deceased family members; this gives me a way to distinguish between the two.

The practice of nature veneration and ancestor reverence and the traditions thereof form a system that should by no means be taken lightly. There are many books on the market for those of you who would like a more in-depth view on this subject; however, by reading this book and following just a few simple suggestions, you can begin your journey towards higher awareness and the fulfillment of your soul.

"PRAYER"

"Prayer is the means by which the conviction that God is becomes instilled. God becomes, through prayer, a living force in the life of man. The real conviction that God is, comes to man not by belief that there is a God in the outer world, but in the realization of the Divine within himself; and this realization is attained through prayer...Prayer generates a moral force which not only changes lives, but the lives of others also."[9]

CHAPTER 4

DIMINISHING OF THE VOODOO MENTALITY

There is a voodoo mentality in the world that needs to change. Many people think that rituals, ceremonies, or candle burning can be dismissed as voodoo, hoodoo, or juju, and anyone who even tampers with these types of spiritual systems or devotion should be considered evil, a voodoo worker, or in some cases, a witch. This is what has been termed the voodoo mentality. Many individuals use the word voodoo with scorn and disdain, putting it into a negative context to refer to something evil or malicious acts, but the word voodoo derives from the word vodoun, which means "spirit" or the "spirit is present." Vodoun teaches that we must recognize spirit in everything that we do. In every thought and in every action; the spirit is alive.

Vodou (this is the original spelling) is not hoodoo or juju, even though these words are used interchangeably by the uninformed. The word hoodoo is a term or a nickname used loosely to describe rootwork or witchcraft in a negative context; however, hudu (this is the original Ewe spelling) is rooted in Afrikan ritual and magical religious practices, which are used mainly for healing and protection, whereas

Afrikan witchcraft (practiced by women) and sorcery (practiced by men) have the sole purpose of being evil in nature. "Rootwork, or what many have come to be known as hoodoo, taken out of its original context, is a spiritual system born in the areas of the southern United States— Louisiana, the Carolinas, and Florida—and is based on Afrikan slave traditions mixed with a bit of Christianity, Judaism, Paganism, and Native Amerikan Shamanism. Hoodoo of the Amerikas (rootwork) is not a religion, nor is it considered religious, even though it can adapt to any one of many religious formations, like Christianity or Judaism."[4]

"For root workers, known today as hoodoo workers, there are no governed structures or levels of hierarchy; it is more an individualistic study and practice of botany—herbs, roots, and minerals—blended with beliefs of myths and legends from many cultures, pagan and non-pagan alike, to spiritually manipulate the outcome of a person's circumstance for either good or evil using supernatural means. Hoodoo practices are normally handed down from a practitioner or from an elder family member or teacher, with no need for initiation or ceremony."[5]

On the other hand, vodou, totally different from hoodoo, represents a legitimate religion. It is a spiritual/religious system that derived from the traditions of the Afrikan slaves and upholds customary structures, levels of hierarchy, ethics, restrictions, and taboos; ceremonial initiations are mandatory. To truly understand our Afrikan spiritual background and heritage, we must first understand the origins of our ancestors and the extent of the slave trade, known as the Middle Passage.

Information about the slave trade varies so much that it is truly hard to pinpoint how many people were savagely taken from their homes, but we do know that the estimated numbers are staggering: somewhere between fifteen and sixty million. For at least four centuries, people were herded onto ships and dispersed all over the so- called New World as slaves. They were taken from various tribes and from various parts of Afrika, primarily West and West-Central Afrika. While most of us are familiar with the millions who were captured from Yorubaland, the Fon, the Nupe, and the Ibo, known as current- day Nigeria, Toga, and Gabon, there were millions more who were captured from the Kongo-Angola region, known today as Angola and the Republic of the Kongo. Others also came from Alkans or the Gold Coast, which is contemporary Ghana. And smaller percentages were captured from places like the Blight of Benin, the Wolof, the Fulbe, the Serer, and the Senegambian. The important point here is to recognize that the enslaved Afrikans sold to North Amerika came from a wide variety of ethnic backgrounds. The larger percentages of slaves were sold to Caribbean areas like Brazil, Cuba, Haiti, Jamaica, Puerto Rico, and Trinidad.

Can you imagine millions and millions of Afrikans (many who were priests and priestesses) from various ethnic backgrounds, all mixed together with their different languages, lifestyles, cultures, spiritual/ religious systems, and cosmologies trying to live cohesively? Sound chaotic and confusing? However, in spite of the language barriers and cultural differences, the slaves found ways to communicate and forge together, and while doing so, they realized that they had basic principles in common. For instance, many of them believed in one Supreme Being, dozens of lesser gods, ancestors, taboos, and the importance of good morals for the well-being of community. All of these common convictions provided a natural comfort level between them and helped them forge ahead in supporting one another.

In vodou, anthropologists have found that its religious base predates Christianity by well over ten thousand years, provoking many misconceptions about its origins and practices. Many of us are led to believe that Haiti was vodou's original birthplace; however, researchers believe, and devotees say, that the true origin of vodou is the nation of Benin, once known as Dahomey. Mami Wata Vodoun Amengansie Chief Priestess, Vivian Hunter-Hindrew, MEd (aka Mama Zogbe), a historian in her own right, explains the following:

> Vodoun, today, is practiced all over West and Central Africa, and originated in East Africa, namely Egypt, Nubia, Ethiopia, Northern India, ancient Ionia (now Greece), and ancient Mesopotamia, where African matriarchal traditions were the dominate force throughout the entire world. As patriarchy (male dominance) became prominent in Africa, and these matriarchal groups were subjugated, and constantly invaded (their democratic/theocratic governments being overthrown by their own men and outsiders), they were forced to migrate West where they and fragments of their ancient religions, such as "Vodoun," remain today.

As stated previously, millions of Afrikans were captured and forced onto slave ships from many, many parts of Afrika, bringing with them their numerous religious traditions, including vodou in its true form, different from what we know as Haitian voodoo, New Orleans voodoo, or Southern voodoo. Afrikan—or better yet, Dahomey—vodou is based on some form of ancestor and nature reverence and, in its pure form, is not mixed or mingled with Catholicism at all. However, Haitian voodoo, New Orleans voodoo, and all other New World voodoo derivatives do have traces of Catholicism as an ingredient in their religious structure, but this could not be helped.

Once the slaves arrived in the New World, they tried, to the best of their livelihood in the face of persecution, to remain true and pure to their original traditions and beliefs, but for the sake of survival, the slaves did what was necessary to save whatever traditions they had left, even if that meant hiding their beliefs behind Catholicism, incorporating Catholicism in some way to improvise, going underground to practice more discreetly, restructuring their practices, modifying their rituals, or using whatever ingredients they could get their hands on. They used what they could and did what they must to save their lives and beliefs, no matter the cost. Afrikans and non-Afrikans with common convictions came together, provoking the creation of the many New World religious/spiritual systems that we know of today, such as Haitian vodou, Santeria, Macumba, Candomblé, etc.

In my search to gain additional knowledge on the term voodoo, I stumbled across an article on the internet called "Vodoun (Voodoo): The Religious Practices of Southern Slaves in America, a History of Religious Persecution and Suppression" by Mami Wata Vodoun Amengansie Chief Priestess, Vivian Hunter-Hindrew, MEd, which speaks about the mentality of this sacred and magical craft primarily developed in many parts of the South. Read the following excerpt:

On many southern plantations, it was even against the law for any enslaved African to pray to their God. The slave owners greatly feared the spiritual powers that many enslaved African priests possessed. Those who were caught praying to God were often brutally penalized, as the following excerpt taken from Peter Randolph's 1893 narrative "Slave Cabin to the Pulpit" recounts:

"In some places, if the slaves were caught praying to God, they were whipped more than if they had committed a great crime. The slaveholders will allow slaves to dance, but do not want them to pray to God. Sometimes, when a slave, on

43

being whipped, calls upon God, he is forbidden to do so, under threat of having his throat cut, or brains blown out. Oh, reader! This seems very hard—that slaves cannot call on their Maker, when the case most needs it. Sometimes the poor slave takes courage to ask his master to let him pray, and is driven away, with the answer, that if discovered praying, his back will pay the bill."

"As a result, an aggressive campaign was implemented to do away with African traditional religious practices once and for all. Heavy fines were often levied. Brutal forms of torture, severe beatings, and even death were imposed on anyone caught practicing any form of the religion. Stringent laws were passed to prevent the Africans from speaking any African languages, building shrines, making ritual drums, or any musical instruments. Family members and neighbors were encouraged to "report" one another if caught practicing any form of the religion. These draconian laws (which continued unabated until well after Reconstruction) included prohibitions against organizing in public; and any other method by which the slave owners suspected they might be "working" their magic. Many priests and priestess' were murdered, some escaped up North, and nearly all who refused to [later] "convert" to Christianity and could not escape, suffered intense spiritual alienation and anguish due to the neglect of their Ancestors and gods. Thousands resisted and continued their practices underground. Forcing a once historically open and proud religio-cultural tradition to develop the underserved reputation of being "dark and sinister" in the West. These medieval and unconstitutional laws were so successful that in less than one generation, the many priests and priestesses who were not murdered were forced to practice underground, and the new generations of enslaved Afro-diaspora had developed a learned afro-hagiophobia: a pathological fear and irrational intimidation of African spiritual and esoteric science, ancestral veneration, and its ritual and cultural expressions. The simplest spirit manifestations that were once understood in their cosmological context now "spooked" the newly conditioned generations of African-Americans.

This relentless campaign of maligning and actively suppressing African religions continued throughout the decades by the colonial [and later United States] government. Replete with its racist imagery, and demeaning Hollywood stereotypes, "Voodoo" became the universal standard by which Christian evangelicals, racist anthropologists, educators, and the general public used to clump, classify, and categorically dismiss all African religious systems under colorful pejorative labels as "evil, crazed, sex-frenzied, idolatrous, cannibals, primitive, fetish worshiping, superstitious, demonic cults" devoid of any meaningful moral foundation, social structure, or philosophical/esoteric content. Intentionally, mocked as "Voodoo," no clear distinctions were made between the ancestral religious traditions and its beneficent practices, and the "darker" maleficent traditions such as "sorcery, conjuration, and witchcraft"; tantamount to the spiritual-genocidal equivalency of blending Satanism with Christianity proper.

Because the African Diaspora welded no significant economic or political clout, and most of what remained of its priesthood duly maligned and discredited, it became nearly impossible to present the true spiritual reality of what Vodou actually is, and its profound importance to the spiritual sustenance of the African Diaspora. Ancestral and spirit "callings" that manifested in their traditional modes went unheeded, many lacking the philosophical/ ritual knowledge and expertise to tend to them. This would often escalate and deteriorate into mental illness, family dysfunction, drug addiction, violent outbursts, alcoholism, suicide, and other forms of self-destructive behavior. Even today, much of the ongoing social malaise, psychic and mental confusion, and spiritual pathology that many in the Diaspora are experiencing, may be directly related to their dis-connectedness from the very gods and ancestors who are inextricably connected to their soul and psyche, but many have now, through centuries of conditioning, ignorance, fear, and shame, learned to mock and avoid. Many try unsuccessfully to seek solace in other Western spiritual practices and Eastern traditions, with little understanding of the reasons why they have found no home or peace."[6]

As you can see, the same old paranoid fears and slave indoctrinating notions that transcended time still exist today, especially amongst our Amerikan born. Therefore, it is my knowing that because of ignorance and past-life programming, people cannot understand that a hoodoo worker or witch can be a spiritualist, herbalist, gifted being, or someone capable of producing anything good; naturally, they fear. And because of that fear, they feel that anyone with the ability to cure, heal, or commune with nature, animals, and the invisible world is weird; therefore, they judge, condemn, and in many cases of the past, they arrested, tortured, burned, hanged, and persecuted anyone accused of practicing so-called witchcraft. Sadly, in some places around the world, the same disapproval exists—even today.

Yet through it all, the ancestral spirits continue to call to our souls. Our ancestors are very cunning, especially when they seek and desire our greatest attention, particularly in family lines of nonbelievers. In these cases, the ancestors find very resourceful ways of obtaining satisfaction and acknowledgement through at least one family member. Usually this individual, in my case, me, is very open-minded and intuitive and will naturally gravitate toward and become highly interested or involved in some sort of spiritual or esoteric medium. Somehow, it becomes their responsibility to ensure that the ancestors and the spirit guides/eguns of the family line are appeased and that the messages from beyond are communicated and passed on to others. This is why some of you, including the so-called God-fearing Christians, who, to no avail, try to ignore the ancestral and spirit/soul callings, are pulled and tempted to occasionally seek hoodoo workers, spiritualists, mediums, healers, and readers to satisfy that old-world spiritual craving and to resolve daily problems that cannot be addressed in common church settings for fear of communal and societal rejection. Call it what you may, but for many of you, the urge—that ole hoodoo—burns within your blood, leaving you to feel empty and unsatisfied with your current spiritual or religious upbringing.

In my continued search to further validate my point about the importance of ancestor veneration amongst various cultures, I came across "Clearing Your Ancestral Blocks," an article written by David Furlong in which he talks about the need to grab every opportunity to heal ancestral family lines because we are all linked to the universe through our ancestry. In this article, Mr. Furlong enlightens us with an excerpt from a book called *Karma and Reincarnation* by Dr. Hiroshi Motoyama, Head Priest of the Shinto Tamamitsu sect of Japan, which states:

> *"The parent/child connection manifests as one link in a long chain of ancestral karma that stretches back through time. Your link to your family allows you to be born into that specific line—it is a link that needs to be understood and respected. In*

this modern scientific age it is very difficult for people to accept the fact that they are responsible to their ancestors, that they are actually liable for the actions of their ancestors if the resulting karma has not yet been dissolved. Many find it absurd to think that the actions of an unknown ancestor could possibly have anything to do with what is happening to them today. But time and time again when investigating someone's karma, I find problems that stretch back generations. Their spirit is not just an individual entity, it is also part of the family spirit that births and nurtures it."

Mr. Furlong continues his article, speaking of ancestral patterns that conclude in a way that is similar to what Mami Wata Vodoun Amengansie Chief Priestess says in her article about the living (us) suffering negatively from the dysfunctions and sins of our forefathers and foremothers. Even in the Bible, Numbers 14:18, there is reference to us as children suffering for the sins (wrong doings) of our forefathers, "even unto the third and fourth generations," clearly suggesting how integral the ancestors are to our lives and how we must learn and teach prayer and sacrifice, including the giving of ourselves, to keep us in harmony with our lineage. Mr. Furlong further makes it clear that many cultures, both sophisticated and primitive, pay a great deal of attention to the ancestral family line, proving that this form of worship is one of the most widespread of all religious belief systems.

Specifically in the Amerikas, many of us have been programmed to believe that ancestor reverence is evil. I feel that evil comes in many shapes and sizes: if a person is evil, he or she is evil in heart, and you do not have to practice any particular religion or spiritual system to be labeled as such. There are many evil people in the world, including in our ancestral lines, far worse than any individual who may pray at an altar or make offerings to their ancestors, deities, or spirit guides/eguns. But I cannot deny that there are individuals who use religion and similar spiritual systems for their own selfish, manipulative, and evil purposes. And for those reasons, they contribute to the negativity bestowed upon Lukumi/Yoruba or similar systems in general. We have to acknowledge and accept the fact that there are individuals who will try to dominate other people and destroy people's lives over money, love, power, envy, jealously, ignorance, or trivial reasons; they are simply evil. However, just as there are evil people in the world, in this religion (as in all religions, spiritual systems, professions, and organizations—none are immune) there are also honest, loving, gifted, and sincere people. We must try not to dismiss the good over concerns of the bad because, believe it or not, what goes around comes around—maybe not when we want it to, but it does eventually, even in the afterlife. And be assured that the spirit of justice is always watching, and if you continue doing good things, live by what is "true", God and the good spirits will favorably side with you.

I must admit, though, there are times when it is very hard to deal with evils that are perpetuated, especially by people who are close to you. It took me a while to understand when to fight and when not to. In my experience, it is not always necessary to fight back through spiritual means, because the spirits and God will fight for you with or without your knowing. However, there will be times when the spirits will request a specific work, action, or offering to help defeat the circumstance at hand, and as long as you follow your spirit guides, you will not go wrong. Therefore, as you seek the road of spiritual fulfillment, try to be aware of the many mentalities/personalities that are counterproductive to the true purpose of why we venerate spirits. I have identified a few:

Mentality/Personality A – In this group, take note of the many individuals living outside and within your own community who are miseducated or altogether uneducated when it comes to proper action in general, but especially where spiritualism is concerned. As you venture out, know that *one* person *never* knows it all. Spiritualism is a daily learning process, a continual study, and experiences will vary from person to person. Keep in mind that there are some fundamental rules that you should, for the most part, adhere to in order to ensure the correct guidance, protection, and growth if you choose to follow this system. Do not be afraid to ask questions. Use your God-given common sense and know that you have choices. You do not have to do or get involved in anything that makes you feel terribly uncomfortable or that goes against your principles. In the final analysis, believe and know in your heart that no one can take better care of you than *you*.

Mentality/Personality B – Contrary to popular belief, there are millions of professional people who are actors/actresses, artists, doctors, judges, lawyers, music professionals, nurses, policemen, politicians, professors, radio personalities, scholars, teachers, or just plain old educated, middle-class folks who venerate the ancestors and Òrìsà through some form of Afrikan-based spiritual system. However, individuals in the mentality/personality B group believe that the veneration of nature and our ancestors is primitive and a pastime of the poor. To a degree, this belief has merit when you take into account that the less fortunate are more apt to believe in the mysteries of the unknown and invisible forces that can help alleviate their problems of circumstance—this is their way of keeping faith and hope alive. If you think about it, this is no different from the poor and disadvantaged who believed in Jesus' healings and miracles that are recorded in the Bible. In the Holy Bible, King James Version, book of Luke 5:20-26, Jesus heals a person who was sick with palsy. This case of healing was so astonishing and profound that it led the author of the book of Luke to say, "And they were all amazed, and they glorified God, and were filled with fear, saying, we have seen strange things today."

Jesus' objective was to preach to and save the lost souls of the disadvantaged, the ill, and those of a bad nature. He performed multitudes of healings and miracles as proof of his great power and as a way to gain trust from the people, encouraging them to change the errors of their ways and to turn their lives over to God. However, Jesus acquired fear instead of trust from many around him and was betrayed, arrested, beaten, sentenced to death, and crucified. They could not understand the form of worship he required in his role as the son of the almighty God. To me, it is the same today, just a different time and place. Messages of truth and true spiritual power are as feared today as they ever were. The funny thing is there really is no reason to fear, because we were all born with spiritual gifts. It is just that some people are more open- minded than others.

Mentality/Personality C – Fear is bred by those who lack courage to know the truth about the infinite powers that dwell in the universe and within each individual person. Individuals and initiates who are ignorant, arrogant, insecure, narrow-minded, and stagnant in their states of mind, their views, and their ways of life are in this group. Therefore, they perpetuate lower vibrational and fear-based thinking to those around them. These people are stubborn and egotistical. They think they know everything. They refuse to further their spiritual and/or religious educations with their elders, or they think that they must stay stuck with the same old traditions and values; they are reluctant to change. Such attitudes can be impediments to receiving steady and solid growth.

Another regrettable reality is the existence of spiritualists or initiates who take advantage of the vulnerable, those who are considered the spiritual weaklings of the community. They thrive and feed off the defenseless, who are usually in desperate situations that require immediate attention. Unscrupulous spiritualists take advantage of such easy targets. Most of the negativity stems from spiritualists who are so conflicted and confused within themselves that they create conditions of dominance and submission over their clients in order to feel superior, rather than help change an oppressed mentality to an empowered one that can become more progressive. With the lack of education and knowledge and the lack of open-mindedness and positivity within our own spiritual system, we brand and hurt ourselves, giving opportunities to onlookers to brand and hurt us, in turn. In the end, the unscrupulous spiritualists create additional false perceptions about our traditions of nature and ancestor veneration. Regrettably, the desperately poor economic status of the less fortunate produces discord and misery, which eventually spills over into the community where more harm than good is done towards one another.

And as dissatisfaction with the misguided views, bad conduct, degraded ethics, and unskilled services provided within Afrikan-based spiritual/religious systems increase, there will be a radical transformation in the beliefs and principles of the good and capable individuals involved, driving them to become facilitators of change. It appears to be their destiny to bring new experiences and ideals forth, adding a new dimension to an old way of doing things. It does not mean that they are not loyal and do not see the beauty inherent within the system as it is; they will just integrate and share new concepts and spiritual principles relevant to the ever-increasing changes of the world: socio-economically, physically, materially, and spiritually.

The world is changing; therefore, religion as a whole will have to change with it. Take into account the scientific processes being developed and introduced to us everyday, such as cloning. How will we deal with it on a spiritual level? This is a perfect example of how the mysteries of yesterday are the realities of today, and today's mysteries will become the realities of tomorrow. And as everyday life transforms because of new technologies, ongoing struggles, and ever-changing issues within our environment, we will be forced to tap into the inner depths of our minds and souls to find new and creative ways of living, thereby changing religious views.

Life is changing as we know it, and because we do not know where we are heading, we will be forced to rely on our spirit guides and trust our spiritual processes as the circumstances of the world unfold. We will wholeheartedly need to depend on the invisible realm to supply us with solutions to dilemmas that we have yet to face or have not had to face at all in our communities, similar to the way that we had to deal with the tragic events of 9/11, or the fact that many of us have no experience dealing with our children being drafted to fight wars, not knowing if we will ever see them again. We will need to prepare ourselves for world transformations and become more open and flexible to making changes within our religious structures in the same ways our predecessors had to adapt their traditions to new world views in order to preserve their lives and beliefs.

Furthermore, not only do we need to diminish the negativity and voodoo mentalities projected by outside influences, but we must also diminish the negativity and voodoo mentalities within ourselves by making inward adjustments to self in order to project positivity toward our families and communities. Our own worst enemy is our selfish self. Sometimes we think or assume that things are going wrong in our lives because of spiritual manipulation, witchcraft, bad luck, or a curse. Although this can be true, in many cases the reality is that we are our own worst enemies. We hurt ourselves through poor judgments, negative thinking, and bad timing. We jump into relationships, spend beyond our means, take impulsive actions, and set ourselves up for failure. This happens because we deny and lie to ourselves, perpetuating false truths in hopes of feeling better. We can diminish negatives by learning to find and maintain a sense of balance within. Most of us do not think our plans through, or in many cases, we do not plan at all; we just jump in and set ourselves up for disappointment after disappointment; we lack self awareness. Because we are mentally and emotionally out of control, we attract lives that run out of control. In these instances, it is not a spiritual issue but rather a discipline issue. Because of the misdirection of energy, the universe will sometimes work against us, making us feel powerless and frustrated, all because we have not learned the correct processes needed to live rewarding lives. We should learn how to control and organize our thoughts, emotions, and actions for setting goals and making plans, and at the same time learn how to be practical and how to build solid foundations, which in turn will provide support and stability to our lives, alleviating negative outcomes.

Another huge energy that affects how we all exist in this life is the universe—the alignment of the planets, the stars, the sun, and the moon. In other words, astrology. It determines the way universal energies flow through us, such as making us too aggressive or not aggressive enough. The challenge is to find the proper balance in our personalities and emotions. The universe takes us through alterations, working as spirit through us and affecting our inherent personalities and behaviors. And because of these universal energies, we were born with innate strengths and weaknesses, making life sometimes easy and sometimes difficult, depending on the day, time, and location of our entry into this world. To add to the complexity, sometimes these universal energies are at odds with each other; our feminine and masculine energies demonstrate this. This struggle may affect how we communicate and interact with others in general.

For instance, one of the reasons it used to be hard for me to maintain a romantic relationship is because masculine energy dominated within my personality. I was overly independent, domineering, argumentative, and combative; these are all male traits that may intimidate and challenge men. In the early part of my life, these traits operated through me as a necessary strength, only because this was the energy I needed to survive harsh circumstances that I've dealt with as I grew up and throughout my life. But now, that masculine energy has become more of a weakness and blockage, only because it is no longer essential for me to use these traits. Not that I will need to get rid of these traits altogether, but at this point, it has become fundamental for me to put those traits on the back burner. My challenge now is to become less aggressive, judgmental, and combative and more balanced by working with my feminine-creative side. My objective is to learn how to complement the masculine energy inherent within the male sex, which will ultimately make it easier to have a healthy and balanced relationship with a man, providing that I have learned from my past mistakes and choose the right kind of mate to begin with. Astrology has helped me understand this issue.

Clearly, our problems are not always spiritual in the way we might think of them, and to be fair to the spiritual realm, the spirits are not the ones that always affect our lives—whether for good or bad. Our issues are, for the most part, either inherent or self-inflicted. Therefore, how the spirit realm influences us—whether positively or negatively—depends on how we handle the strengths and weaknesses that are inherent within us. Most of the time we humans hate to be criticized, but we must learn that through awareness of our weaknesses we have greater power to control and redirect negative or misguided energy. In return, we learn to balance the physical, material, and spiritual aspects of our lives.

You see, all these things, whether physical, material, mental, emotional, or spiritual, work hand in hand. Religion, spirit guidance, and astrology simply provide insight into who we are and how we interact within our communities. Through forms of spiritualism and working with our ancestors and spirit guides, we become empowered to make proper changes or better choices during our walks on earth. Unfortunately, human nature causes us to have to learn our greatest life lessons through pain and suffering. But to truly understand ourselves and to truly understand the spirit realm and how it influences our lives, we must gain additional understanding of the universe, planetary influences, and nature, because everything tangible or intangible, whether seen or unseen, exists through some realm of energy that resides within universal boundaries.

By learning about nature and its energetic properties and forces, we learn how to better equip ourselves to move gracefully through life—whether we have to work hard or we have greater ease as our birthright. This includes learning the source of our problems and learning how to deal with our obstacles and challenges, and in turn being taught which force of nature (which guardian spirit or Òrìsà [nature deity]) to work with to help us relieve our suffering. For example, if you were a farmer and your crops did not flourish because the land was in a dry condition, you would need to appease the Spirit of Rain. Trying to appease any other force of nature just would not help the situation.

In order to diminish negativity, we must change our mentalities so they are much more purposeful. This can be done by analyzing our inner selves, adjusting our egos, raising our consciousnesses, along with, working with a religious/ spiritual cultivating system that serves as a vehicle and guide for living well, a system that nurtures and provides growth within a group of individuals with common spiritual and religious goals. And now, with technology on our side and the ability to access high volumes of data within seconds, the knowledge of spirit veneration will gradually grow and become filled with professionalism, intellectual discipline, in-depth education, health consciousness, creativity, heightened awareness, and appropriate economic gain for both individuals and communities all around the world. With that happening, and as our knowledge base broadens, we will be required to study other cultures and other ways of living to find additional answers that are not always right in front of us.

We must all realize that every culture holds a piece of the puzzle, and every culture owns a piece of God, whoever or whatever God is or is perceived to be. In return, many practitioners will strive to grow in knowledge and understanding to provide the education necessary to help others live better in consciousness, teaching them how to properly embrace spiritualism and to reconnect with spirits, the ancestors, and the Creator, portraying the true concepts and purposes of this faith as a way of life and not some gloried religious fad of a superficial way of living. My ultimate wish is to witness the enhancement of credibility, acceptance, and respect for all devotees of this beautiful yet misunderstood faith of ancestor and nature/Òrìsà veneration.

FOR THIS I PAY HOMAGE

By Oba Ilari Aladokun

I call upon the ancestors of my fathers and forefathers and of my mothers and foremothers for their inspiration and the renewal of my own spirit. It is in their honor that I make offerings and pour libations. It is in their honor that I give thanks for everything facilitated on the backs of my ancestors. And for this I pay homage.

As I call upon their force, I honor their contributions, convictions, and dignity. And as they etch the horrible atrocities of history into my mind, I welcome these recollections, for I must never forget. I must remember never to repeat that history but to develop and grow through knowledge and admiration for the strides they made throughout history, despite adversity. And for this I pay homage.

I call upon the creative spirit of my ancestors to teach me the ways and cultures of the old in this new time, and I welcome their memories of the past, for knowing the past, I know myself. And for this I pay homage.

I call upon my ancestors as I walk the paths they once walked. They will walk before me, leaving their prints for me to follow, and I will avoid those old roads of traps and pitfalls only to encounter a new road, bringing me steps closer to victory and freedom. And for this I pay homage.

And in honor of the creator, I commemorate my ancestors through prayers and rituals, that I may become a facilitator of their great wisdom, courage, and dedication, impressing upon the world their ingenious contributions to humanity. AND FOR THIS I PAY HOMAGE. Àṣe o!

GOD IN ME

My first love is God and God in me. And to love me is to love God. Be good to me: help me, nurture me, protect me, and you will be rewarded the same from God and God in me. Give praise unto his holy name.

My body is my temple, painted in a beautiful color—a temple of holiness, God's home. If you don't like my color, then you don't like the color of God. God made me in his image. God's in me.

My heart pumps scarlet red, same as yours—God gave me this heart. So why hurt me? 'Cause in doing so, God surely hurts, too.

My gift to you is love, giving and helping, for this is my way—God's way. So to take advantage of me is to take advantage of God. Hear what I say.

My eyes are the window to my soul, so why show me so much pain? Disrespect, condemnation, neglect—but didn't you know? God's waiting for my soul and now it is stained.

And when you finished with me, you didn't even clean or shine me up before God called me back! Now I have to see my father in shame, as if I were an ole rundown shack.

And you say you know God. In God you trust, that is what you say. But I don't think so; 'cause if you did, you wouldn't have abused me, cursed me, nor used me in such a way. For now I worry, what will God think? My pride didn't want me to be seen—dirty, soiled, and unclean!

So take my advice, for God taught me to forgive; reevaluate your relationship with God and God in me. God made me in his image. God's in me.

— Words inspired from those on the other side
By Oba Ilari Aladokun

LOVE MATTERS

"*Love is a divine power in the Universe. It is advisable that a conscientious awareness and vigilance be exerted so that its application is not deviated from its accurate or proper use.*

When an individual dedicates himself solely to accumulating riches or hoarding his wealth, this intense determination and excessive energy expended is referred to as "greed." The same holds true, when the individual is possessive in every and all things.

When his personal surroundings, his home, or living quarters entirely become the center of his universe, he displays "egoism."

When he finds reason to praise or boast about his possessions, his accomplishments, his superior intelligence, yet undermining the value or feelings of other, this is considered "envy," as well.

Apostle Paul, in his writings to the lovable Phillippian community, made a remark of a profound significance. He assures us that love abounds more and more in knowledge and depth of insight, so that the apprentice can fully appreciate the things that are excellent."

Let us instruct ourselves and through observing and scrutinizing our personal actions and by studying our own failings, in order to improve our understanding. Let us attempt to educate ourselves in order to achieve the more and intellectual enhancement, imperative for our improvement through which we will have the possibility of manifesting the sublime love that brings us closer to God..."[xii]

CHAPTER 5

SPIRIT GUIDES
"WE ARE NOT ALONE!"

The concept of death and an invisible world is very complicated. I will give you a synopsis of my understanding of life on the other side; the majority of my knowledge comes from several years of study and experience working with the spirits alone and within groups, through spirit communications and dreams, and through initiation into two spiritual systems. I have acquired additional knowledge from various books that have given clarity to my many encounters. I will do my best to share the world on the other side, within which our ancestors, our guardians, and other spirit entities exist. This way, when you speak to them you will have a clearer understanding of how they can assist you in your everyday life.

"We are not alone!" I use this phrase not to speak about aliens, but to speak about entities or beings that share the complexities of this universe alongside us. Within our universal sphere there are energetic forces of various frequencies that are both positive and negative in nature. A vast portion of this energy is in the form of spirit beings. In nature, everything originates in spirit, thus making it easy

for us to tap into its essence to gain a higher understanding and awareness of our Creator's infinite love and power.

This brings me to the spirit world, which is made up of several astral planes. The makeup of the spirit world is complex, but note that not all spirits need to go through these steps exactly as stated; some will ascend to their appropriate realm according to their deeds or frequency level. For clarity and easier understanding, I have opted to discuss and divide the spirit world into planes or levels.

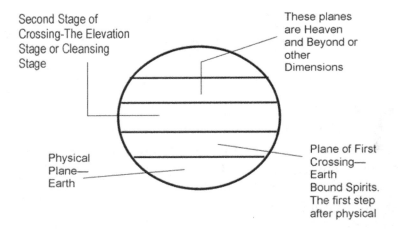

Second Stage of Crossing-The Elevation Stage or Cleansing Stage

These planes are Heaven and Beyond or other Dimensions

Physical Plane— Earth

Plane of First Crossing— Earth Bound Spirits. The first step after physical

The bottom half of the circle represents the physical plane, the plane of the living, the here and now—earth.

The next is the plane of the first crossing, the first step after physical death. This is the lower level, which contains the spirits that remain closest to us. These are people who have died and left their bodies behind, but have carried with them some essence of who they were on earth. Many of these spirits have the same characteristics and personalities as when they were alive—goodness to malice, intelligence to ignorance.

Spirits who linger in this realm are called "earthbound" spirits. A variety of spirits who have not accepted their physical deaths and try to hold on to their physical appearances and material ways of life live in this plane. Many of these spirits do not even realize that they are dead, especially the newly expired or those who have experienced sudden or tragic deaths. Others know that they are dead but linger around because of their loved ones. They feel that they have not fulfilled their obligations in life while other spirits linger around seeking vengeance.

Spirits on this level can affect our lives for good or bad. The bad or malignant spirits are those who have not desired to advance/elevate their souls to a higher plane, either by choice or ignorance. They are considered spirits of darkness, entities that were of a bad nature in the physical world and have crossed over with the same characteristics and intentions as when they were alive. These entities try to deceive, cause havoc, and disrupt our lives for sheer amusement, for revenge, or as a way to force us to acknowledge the pain and suffering once bestowed upon them. As they feel tormented, they want to torment us, and as they feel miserable, they want us to be just as miserable.

Be aware of malevolent or inferior spirits that can attach themselves to you in many ways and for many reasons. One way is through foul play, when an individual has used and sent a bad spirit to you to purposely disrupt your life for selfish or evil reasons. Remember, these spirits are already dark and vengeful in nature so they will gladly take on the task. You can also pick up and attract a bad entity without knowing. Some of the most common reasons are that eguns/spirits are attracted to the thoughts, energies, or emotions that we project, such as negative or perverse thinking, sadness, depression, loneliness, or fits of anger. Bad or tormented spirits can follow you from a past life (incarnation). Even your personality type can and will attract low vibrational spirits. There are even malevolent or inferior eguns/spirits that will try to sleep with you or have sex with you. Sometimes this occurs when an egun/spirit thinks that you are its mate, husband, or wife possibly from a past life. Other times, the egun/spirit could think that it is in love with you and, in a worst-case scenario, there could be an egun/spirit that is simply evil and wants to take advantage and force itself on you. These situations are extreme and usually happen if you are spiritually and emotionally vulnerable and weak. Remember bad/evil spirits are attracted to our vulnerabilities.

Many times, if you are aware, you can feel when something unnatural is affecting you, whether you are sleeping or awake, because you will not feel like yourself. Some of the common symptoms include feeling a heaviness, like bricks weighing on your shoulders; suffering from sluggishness; experiencing confusion; feeling out of sorts; having a loss of memory; experiencing tiredness; undergoing unusual amounts of illness; encountering insurmountable obstacles; having attitude changes; and on and on. This is why it is extremely important that you continually keep your mind positive, say prayers often, and keep your aura and your living space spiritually clean. If done a regular basis, eventually you will automatically know when something is off or out of balance and if there is foul play involved. And in a case where your own cleansings are not helping to alleviate negativity, or the energy from a bad egun/spirit persists, you will need to seek out a spiritual advisor or medium who is an expert at removing these sorts of energies.

Then there are those spirits who are considered inferior entities only because they may be scared, confused, misguided, or even a little manipulative and mischievous, but they are not necessarily bad or evil. Many of these spirits act out the same as children do when they do not get a good dose of love, affection, or attention. They just need guidance and light, for they do not have the knowledge, courage, power, or strength to elevate their souls to a higher realm.

They remain stuck in this plane until they figure their way out, until help comes along through a spirit helper of greater light, or until—through our prayers and light—they advance and cross over onto a higher plane.

This brings us to the next level, the second level. This part of the circle is the level of cleansing or light and progression. In Spanish communities, they call this *luz y progresso*. This is where the spirit begins shedding old ways of physical existence and gives up appearance, material possessions, and bad habits. When spirits accept this transition, they begin preparing themselves for the next step of evolution to a more purified and enlightened realm.

Ancestors and guardian spirits from higher realms, heaven and beyond, only work within a divine order or with a divine agenda. Spiritual bodies from higher realms have greater frequency levels. The higher the frequency, the more powerful and intelligent they are. Sometimes these heavenly bodies do not visit the lower realms unless necessary. To carry out an assignment, they will contract an inferior spirit. Take a place of employment, for example; you rarely see the president of a company making copies unless there is no choice. Instead, a clerk carries out the task. And when necessary, spirits will also band together as a team to carry out a particular assignment that requires additional energies or skillfulness. The spirit world operates in a manner similar to the workplace. Because inferior spirits have not relinquished their material forms or material ways of physical existence, they have many of the same abilities that they had while on earth—we just cannot see them. They can make noises, move things, or make things fall over, and more often than not, this is their way of trying to get our attention. Because many of them continue to hold onto their old ways, they will take concerns and issues into the afterlife with them. They can suffer and be affected by cold, hunger, thirst, pain, depression, and happiness, or hold grudges, the same as we do.

No matter the level of hierarchy, spirits have many different skills, specialties, and accomplishments, but many individuals have a misconception that spirits can do anything and everything for us. Believe it or not, spirits do have limitations, for they only help us with the things with which we cannot help ourselves. Their limitations can occur for a number of unknown reasons, but I tend to think that timing, their frequency level, their skillfulness in handling the issue at hand, and universal/natural laws are amongst the many reasons for limitations. Depending on our deeds and our persistence, they will go beyond the limits to overcome the hurdles for us and in order to do so, they may seek assistance from a higher being, work with others as a team, or work harder and longer until the goal is accomplished. When this is done, it strengthens and increases the frequency level of that spirit, which in turn gives them the ability to do things that other spirits cannot do. As stated before, higher frequency equals greater power, clarity, and intelligence. For instance, some spirits can walk through walls and some cannot. Sounds strange, huh? This is why, at times, many of us will hear a knock at the door, open it, and no one is there. The spirit had to knock in order to enter.

On each realm, there are lessons to be learned and tests to pass. These realms are filled with teachers as well as spirit schools, where spirits can learn and advance themselves. Just like we in the living graduate through levels of education and skill sets, spirits who want to advance do the same. They learn what they need and they advance on. Those that have accepted death and have elevated to higher levels each attain a purpose, and they are considered superior spirits or spirits on a high order. Many of these spirits have acquired the power to travel back and forth through many different realms, even down to the first one nearest us, where they can teach, protect, and provide for us.

Often, spirit guides also have the distinct purpose of testing us. They will mix and mingle with spirits from the lower realms and, in doing so; they will disguise themselves or take on characteristics of another spirit or undesirable living person. For example, a guide may take the disguise of a homeless person, an addict, or a handicapped person just to test our compassion. That is why we have the phrase, "Be nice to everyone, for they just might be an angel." These divine entities mask themselves, because they know that if we know who they truly are, we will be on our best behavior. Thus, even the good and purposeful spirits will try to trick us for our own good.

I remember an encounter I had about two years ago while driving in New York City. I stopped at a red light and this filthy, drunk-looking old man came up to my car and asked for change. If you know anything about New York City, you know not to roll down your window to give anybody anything, let alone money. But I was compelled to give him a dollar. When he noticed what I had given him, he was ecstatic, as if I had given him a $100 bill. He immediately began to bless me. I will never forget his exact words. "Thank you, thank you, thank you. May God bless you 100 times over." He kept directing good fortunes at me, and he touched my heart in such a way that I wanted to cry.

I could have decided not to give the dollar, thinking that he would just go and buy more liquor or wine with it, but that was not the point. The point was that I sincerely gave somebody who was less fortunate than I something I was in a position to give. For all I know, this could have been a test, and he could have been an angel in disguise. Even if he was not, his blessings still may have been heard and will come into my life when least expected.

Many of our guides have been with us from our births. Spiritual domains/tribes (groups of spirit guides) will vary from person to person. We have our own spirit domains/tribes that include ancestors and spirit guides/eguns that are assigned to assist us during our lives, helping us work towards our destinies. These guides can be of a masculine or feminine energy, of various ethnicities, and from various time frames, usually the time of their last incarnation. We can have the same spirit guide throughout our lives or several spirit guides, each with a divine purpose of teaching and helping us learn the lessons we need to learn during this incarnation.

In my culture, there are several names used to identify a spirit guide/egun or guides that may be walking with a person. Some common names are Gypsy/Hitana, Congo or Negro, Madama, or Indian/Indio. Your spirit domain/tribe can consist of one of the above, all of them, or any combination thereof, including many others not listed, like a slave, a priest, a nun, a pirate, an Arab, an Asian, a vampire, a famous activist, a fairy—the list goes on. Any one of these aforementioned spirit guides/eguns can be the head or chief in charge of all the others that may dwell in your spirit domain. This principal guide/egun is usually elevated, positive in nature, intelligent, and comes with light and knowledge to help you during your evolutionary process.

What makes a spirit tribe interesting is that you can be an Afrikan-Amerikan with a guide of Asian descent as your principal guardian spirit, with no prejudices from the spirit realm. But many times humans have problems with this. For instance, when I found out that I had to appease my white ancestors who were trying to help me, I rebelled like hell. I said, "No way!" No disrespect to anyone, but at that time all I could think about was how "whitey" treated my Afrikan ancestors, and there was no way I would pay homage or give offerings to my white ancestors. Then, as time went on, people explained that because of my white ancestors, who were Irish, I was able to accomplish many things that I otherwise would not have been able to accomplish. My Irish ancestors were giving me luck and blessings, and those ancestors were now helping me by making right what they failed to do when they were alive. It may have been wrong of me to feel this way, but I looked at it as a sort of retribution. That made it easier to handle.

Our spiritual guardians love us, but sometimes they are our harshest critics, and as much as we might not like it, it is their job to be this way. I know firsthand about difficult guardians because I have many, but one in particular was the first of my guardians to make his presence known to me, which he did about sixteen years ago, and we have fought many battles together. My guardian does not make life easy for me at all. He keeps me on my toes. He makes me work very hard, both physically and spiritually. He does not let me get lazy, and if I don't do what I am supposed to do, sometimes he may let things happen to me just so that I can learn my lesson. His teachings are very raw, never sugar-coated. For many years, I never understood why he was so difficult, and in spiritual readings, many people have seen him as very difficult, mean, and rebellious, but it was not until recently that he revealed why he is the way he is.

One day, while I was ironing, he revealed to me that I am a warrior in training and that he is hard on me to strengthen me. Everything that I have achieved in life I have had to fight for, even when it came time for me to be initiated. Nothing has ever been given to me, nor has anything ever been easy. And in looking back on my life, I know that one of my lessons in this lifetime is to learn how to fight and protect what I have. I must learn courage and discipline, and he knows that if I can deal with his harshness and all the issues that he throws my way, I will be able to deal with the harshness of the world in general. He made it very clear that I would gain his full respect only when I gain the respect of the world.

For whatever reason, this spirit who was assigned to me has the kind of energy that is necessary for me to get through this lifetime, and in knowing this, I have no choice but to welcome the challenges. Our guardians will test our loyalties, our convictions, our strengths, our weaknesses, our hearts, and, above all, our faith. They know us very well, and they know if we can or cannot handle situations. They know if we have the kinds of characters that embody pure laziness or if we have the kinds of characters that are made up of sheer determination. Most of the time we are our own worst enemies, and many times we do not have the confidence in ourselves to handle situations or carry out tasks that we know we are capable of performing. And in these situations, we blame our guardians for not helping us when our own shortsightedness leads us to outcomes we do not like. It is similar to blaming our guardians for being in debt. The fact that we are way over our heads in bills comes from our own misguided and uncontrolled behavioral patterns of unconscious, impulsive, and brash spending. We cannot blame the credit card companies, the bill collectors, or the spirit guides for our irresponsible spending habits. The spirit guides did not get us into our messes, yet we look to them for miracles—like hitting the lottery—to get us out. Sorry, Charlie, it does not work that way. We cannot blame our guardians—we can only blame *ourselves*.

The other thing that some people do is measure their lives and faith by material gains. These are people who think that they are struggling and not doing well, and they continually ask themselves, "Why should I pray or appease my ancestors and spirit guides/ eguns, or do anything, when I am struggling so hard?" And for this thoughtless reason, they blame God and the guardians, and make every selfish excuse to worship less or not at all, when in actuality they have everything but are ungrateful, miserable, and never satisfied. If one little thing happens that affects their lifestyle in their superficial way of thinking, they fall out like spoiled brats, all because things are not happening the way they want them to happen.

God and the spirit guides give us what we *need*, not necessarily what we *want*. However, and to be fair to those who are legitimately struggling day-to-day, know that sometimes it may be a part of our destiny to work hard and fight for everything that we receive in life; this happens to be my road, but it is not something that I can blame on God or my guides. I just have to hold my head up high, make better choices and decisions, take responsibility for my life and actions, and pray to God and my guides that I make it through with as little pain and struggle as possible. Remember, our guardians cannot walk for us; we must take the necessary steps and approaches to accomplish our goals. They can only steer us around the obstacles or give us additional options and routes to reach our goals; it is up to us, not them, to make every effort to succeed.

Many times our guardians will not help us right away; they will sit back and see if we are going to make the first move, or they will look to see what solutions we will come up with on our own. This approach helps us build our characters and our psyches, discouraging us from becoming dependent upon their help. In this way, we learn to help ourselves and to think for ourselves. As we build character and develop the ethics for living decent lives, we better equip ourselves for the material world, as well as for the spiritual world. We put our ancestors and guardians in better positions to aid us in our everyday lives. And each time we pass a test or do something generous without prejudice, we not only help ourselves elevate and evolve, but we also help them. We are in the movie that they are watching. They have learned not only from their own past experiences, but they are learning from our fortunes and misfortunes as well, diligently trying to keep us from making the same mistakes they made. But ultimately, it is up to us to open ourselves to their love and to follow their guidance.

"We shall eventually have to accept responsibility for every thought, word and deed we beget and re-experience exactly whatever suffering we have caused...Every act, thought and choice adds to a permanent mosaic; our decisions ripple through the universe of consciousness to affect the lives of all...Even if one sits isolated in a cave, his thoughts influence others whether he wishes it or not. Every act or decision you make that supports life supports all life, including your own. The ripples we create return to us. This, which may once have seemed a metaphysical statement, is now established as a scientific fact.

Everything in the universe constantly gives off an energy pattern of a specific frequency which remains for all time and can be read by those who know how. Every word, deed and intention creates a permanent record. Every thought is known and recorded forever. There are no secrets; nothing is hidden, nor can it be. Our spirits stand naked in time for all to see. Everyone's life, finally, is accountable to the universe." - David Hawkins, MD

CHAPTER 6

CHILDREN AND SPIRITS

As we all know, children are sponges for learning, and they are very sensitive. Children are also more intuitive and more instinctually connected to nature and animals than many parents realize. Nothing is too ridiculous, silly, or farfetched to them because their minds, imaginations, and creativity have yet to be conditioned by societal fears, dogma, prejudices, or limitations. Their imaginary friends are often very real, and they can describe these playmates with distinct accuracy. Most children are not afraid of the unknown, and because of their innocence and honesty, it is very easy for spirits to communicate with them. Their minds, hearts, and souls, with some exceptions, are for the most part perfectly aligned with the universe, which leaves them susceptible to various frequencies of spirit contact, positive and/or negative.

Since children are openly connected to the physical and spiritual worlds, they easily experience or absorb the emotions of the people around them. When this happens, children often mistake these emotions as their own, for they have not yet learned how to distinguish between their feelings and those of others. This particularly holds true for children who are susceptible to negative energies from the invisible realm. In most cases, neither the child nor the parent can distinguish between normal misbehavior and behavior influenced by a mischievous entity. And even though I am speaking of children in this section, this has also been proven true for adults. As the parents, we think that our children are purposely misbehaving, but in actuality, children can act out the behavior of inferior spirits. Consider the following story about little Chuck Perkins, as told by his mom, S. Perkins:

"My youngest son, Chuck, is quite the handful and the most rambunctious of my three sons. He is naturally mischievous, very smart, and absolutely loves the outdoors. Chuck tends to get into lots of trouble. He isn't a bad child by any means, just very mischievous! During a misa/ séance about three years ago, a medium asked Chuck if he heard a voice that was telling him that it was okay to do things that he knows could get him into trouble. Chuck was stunned, and the look of disbelief on his face spoke volumes because he had never mentioned this to anybody, not even me, his mother, and he felt relieved to know that it wasn't just him and that he wasn't losing it. He felt so much better that someone else had brought his experience to the light.

He responded by saying that he always hears someone telling him to do things that he knows will get him yelled at, and because a lot of times he actually doesn't get caught, he considers it fun sometimes. Chuck was only about nine years old at that time, and he has since calmed down considerably. He still gets into mischief; however, not nearly as much thanks to the spiritual help that he has received over the years from various spiritualists, priests, and the very author of this book, who is also his godmother!"

Let me clarify: most children are naturally curious and mischievous, and they test our nerves to see what they can get away with, but there are times when that curiosity and mischief are not all their own. Spirits communicate through thought form; they send messages into our minds, and because children's minds are so open, they sometimes listen to these messages and, in return, they act upon what they hear or feel.

This brings me to an interesting point about how children and adults who can see, hear, or feel spirit energy have no understanding about the effects that the spirit world can truly have on them. Because of this, some are diagnosed with mental conditions. Yes, there are children and adults with legitimate medical and psychiatric problems, but I believe that many have mental health problems of a purely spiritual nature. Let's take schizophrenia, for example.

An article on Mentalwellness.com uses the American Psychiatric Association's description of schizophrenia as "one of the most debilitating and baffling mental illnesses known." From a scientific point of view, people with schizophrenia have been found to have imbalances of two brain chemicals: dopamine and serotonin. Dopamine is responsible for our emotions and motivation, and serotonin acts as a messenger and stimulates muscle movement, switching nerves on and off. The article continues by stating that many researchers have found that the majority of schizophrenic patients have suffered from poor parenting or meager willpower. As I further researched schizophrenia, it appeared that patients portray the same types of characteristics that mediums and spiritualists display during spirit contact, séance, spiritual masses, or trance mediumship. Mentalwellness.com lists some of the early warning signs of schizophrenia as:

- Hearing or seeing something that is not there
- A constant feeling of being watched
- Peculiar or nonsensical way of speaking or writing

- Strange posturing
- Deterioration of academic or work performance
- A change in personality
- Increasing withdrawal from social situations
- Irrational, angry, or fearful responses to loved ones
- Inability to sleep or concentrate
- Inappropriate or bizarre behavior
- Extreme preoccupation with religion or the occult

Anyone who is a devotee of Lukumi/Yoruba and has experienced séance and spirit possession or trance mediumship can tell you that they either have experienced the majority of the listed items themselves or have seen the exact same characteristics displayed by spiritualists and mediums all the time. Let's take this one step further: many people do not realize that when they think they are hearing and/or seeing things or being watched, a spirit is trying to gain their attention. The fact that you can possibly hear, see, or feel a spirit entity means that you are spiritually open and connected on some level and are not aware of it. This may also be a sign that you have untapped mediumistic skills that you are unaware of.

As I analyzed the list of schizophrenia warning signs, I realized that when people speak or write in a distinctive way I am reminded of spirit communication through one of the mediumistic skills called automatic writing. Strange posturing, changes in personality, irrational and bizarre behavior, and extreme preoccupation with religion or the occult are all definite signs of spirit contact, spirit trance, or spirit possession experienced in many spiritual systems and mediumship practices. As far as the deterioration of academic and work performance, most children who see and hear spirits, especially in school, have a hard time because they feel that they have nowhere to turn, such as in the story of Miles, which you will read later in this chapter.

Fortunately for Miles, he had an outlet in his mom and his spiritual family. The problem here is awareness. It seems that the only difference between some individuals who are schizophrenic and people who are spiritualists or mediums is how they control the actions, emotions, and thought forms that are being received from a spirit entity. If it is true that schizophrenic patients have weak willpower, then this would mean that they do not know how to control these spirit influences. They are very open and vulnerable, and they cannot differentiate or control these emotions and actions that do not belong to them. This works positively, just as well as negatively. Because we live in a society that does not believe in an invisible world, these sufferers and patients do not even know how to rationalize what is happening to them. Neither they nor their loved ones know how to handle or deal with the situation at hand, so they are perceived and, in many cases diagnosed, as crazy, delusional, irrational, disorganized, and moody.

Again, I am not a doctor, nor am I trying to diminish or negate the fact that there are legitimate mental illnesses caused by conditions that can only be diagnosed by qualified health professionals. However, in the case of schizophrenia, I do wonder how many people are diagnosed with it and have the medical condition, and how many have a spiritual condition. And if it is true that in many cases schizophrenia is caused by poor parenting, then this would suggest that schizophrenia would have had to begin in the younger years of childhood, primarily with children who more than likely suffered issues of abandonment, antisocial behavior, abuse, low self-esteem, lack of compassion or humility, poor self-confidence, rejection, sadness, pain, or hurt. All of these negative feelings, on some level, become the perfect festering playground to attract forces of a negative influence, provoking the child to act and respond in ways that are deemed inappropriate by their community and society. This is why I cannot stress enough the importance of working with children on some kind of spiritual level, even if that means doing something as simple as a prayer.

We watch the news and read the papers, and everyone is asking, "What's wrong with the kids nowadays?" Statistics show that children under the age of fifteen are committing more and more serious crimes: killing, raping, stealing, selling drugs, and prostituting. Who is to blame — the parents, the schools, the churches, society; maybe a combination of all of them? No matter who's to blame, there is definitely a negative energetic force out there that is taking control of our kids. One thing is for certain: we need to be compelled to pray for *all* our children. We must call upon the guardian angels and superior spirits to protect and watch over them when we cannot. No matter the age, *these are our "babies"* and we must teach them not only to pray for themselves, but how to pray for the strength to resist all suggestions with negative content.

If you are having negative experiences with your child, I recommend some sort of spiritual cleansing bath and prayer to cleanse the child's aura of any negative influences (see my section on spiritual baths in Chapter 9). This is a mild but temporary remedy and should not be taken as a substitute for medical or psychiatric advice meant for children with legitimate or significant behavioral or mental disorders.

Many of us do not realize it, but our children must learn how to protect themselves and their souls physically as well as spiritually. We need to teach our children the spiritual ways of the ancient ones, and no matter what our religious orientations, our children need to know that there is a higher being, greater than us and within us that can be called upon in times of need. And in preparing our children to be spiritually responsible, we should direct them to speak with the Creator, their guardian spirits, or spirit protectors, not only when having badly experiences but also to thank them for the good experiences. This way, their guides do not feel as if they are only called upon when times are bad. These practices of acknowledging gifts or blessings, giving thanks, and seeking spiritual help teaches our children and us how to develop nurturing, spiritual relationships with the Creator, ancestors, and guides. If children are guided while young, it will stick with them and become a habit of a lifetime. Even if they stray, they will always know, and be guided back to, the lessons of their roots. Below is a story contributed by S. Perkins, who remembers two very distinct experiences that her son Miles had, one that she became aware of when he was approximately three years old. Here is her story:

When my son Miles was about three years old, we were living in East Harlem, New York, on 120th Street. One day, while washing the dishes, Miles started telling me about his old life—his life in his prior incarnation. Watching me wash the dishes seemed to have sparked a memory that reminded him of his "other mother." He said to me out of nowhere, "My other mother used to do that, too!" referring to my washing the dishes. I was slightly taken aback, but I wasn't startled, nor did I want to startle him. Our conversation went like this:

Miles: *"My other mother used to do that, too!"*

Me: *"Oh really? Who is your other mother?"*

Miles *(very nonchalantly): "She's not here now. She's dead. She died a long time ago."*

Me: *"Oh, okay!"*

Miles: *"She was really nice. She used to read to me, and she would sit with me, too."*

Me: *"Oh, that's so nice."*

Miles: *"But she's gone now. You're my new mommy now,*

and you're nice, too."
Me: *"Well, I'm glad to be your new mommy, but tell me more about your old mommy."*
Miles: *"I don't remember her that well anymore. I could remember a lot before, but now I don't. You're the new mommy now."*
Me: *"Okay, well, that's fine by me."*

That was the first time I knew my son was really my son! I had experienced the same types of things when I was young as well, and I remember fearing being thought of as crazy. After that experience, Miles would often play and converse with spirits that he saw on a regular basis in that apartment. He was particularly fond of a male spirit who had very sad eyes. Miles would pull down on his cheeks to show me how this man looked. He would play with him, talk and laugh with him, etc. One day, I told Miles to tell the man that he had to go into the light. Miles was offended and quickly told me how he didn't want the man to leave and the man was just playing with him because he didn't have anybody else to play with. Needless to say, the man stayed. The lights would turn off and on, all times of the day and night. We would often see the volume buttons on our stereo turn by themselves, and you could hear someone walking through the house when the house was quiet at night while everyone was in bed. Weird things would happen so often that we just came to accept them. Eventually we moved, and the man didn't come with us. We did, however, meet new spirits in our new apartment over the years.

My last story concerning my son's experiences has to do with him actually seeing the dead like you can see your hand. When Miles was thirteen, he went through a Rites of Passage program for his entry into manhood. One of the mentors in the program passed away. I believe he was in a car accident, but I can't remember. At any rate, during this particular time, Miles wasn't doing particularly well in school at all. He could never seem to focus, his concentration was non-existent, and he was edgy and stressed out all the time. One day, he finally decided to tell me that he kept seeing the mentor, who passed away, walking the halls. Miles said that he couldn't tell his friends because they would think that he was crazy. He wanted so badly to tell someone and feared that he couldn't. He said that he felt as if he was going crazy because nobody else had ever shared anything similar. This spirit would look right in the door window of the classroom, smile, and stare at Miles, but most times, he would just walk the halls. I told Miles to tell the mentor that he had to go with his ancestors, to "look for them and not you just because he knows you can see him."

I don't know if Miles told him or not, but eventually he stopped doing poorly in school. Naturally, the first assumption that anyone would make would have been that Miles had a learning disability, had ADD, or was just slow. My mother, Miles's grandmother, would carry on about him needing therapy. No one understood. However, it was my job to assure my son that he wasn't crazy at all, and therapy was the farthest solution from my mind. I tried explaining to my mother, who is normally very open-minded when it comes to the new age, that he didn't need a therapist—he needed a spiritualist! Eventually, I was led to the wonderful spiritual priest, Baba Tony, who helped Miles immensely! To this day, Miles has learned to listen to his spirit guides, and his intuition is amazing. He still sees spirits, but it has toned down considerably with age and training!

When children have the *"gift"* of communing with spirits, we should listen to them cautiously but attentively, for they can sometimes deliver messages from the other side that can contribute to our well-being. Remember that they are children and care should be taken not to force messages out of them or create impossible expectations of them. We do not want them to get turned off, and besides, they can only tell us what the spirits want them to know.

The relationship between spirit and human has to be a

mutual one. I am sure that many of you can recall certain things you saw, dreamt, heard, or felt when you were young, but you did not tell your parents or siblings about them because you feared that they would label you weird or crazy. If we have children, or if there are children around us, we can help them deal with similar experiences if we keep open minds.

One of the jobs of parents is to create environments that are training grounds for children, where they learn right from wrong, problem solving, and freedom of expression, within reason. Among other lessons, children are often told that anything is possible and that they can be whatever they want to be if they believe in themselves. But at the same time, as they grow up and begin to exercise these lessons, obstacles and situations are placed in their paths that may cause disruptions in their connections and abilities to communicate on a spiritual level. If we just dismiss children's experiences and become judgmental and critical, their self-esteem will suffer. Then the children will resort to hiding and suppressing their experiences and/or fears and won't deal with them until adulthood, when the need for guidance may become desperate instead of complementary, making these former children vulnerable to fraudulent spiritualists and mediums who claim they can help. However, if encouraged while young, these former children can develop their abilities and maintain their spiritual connections in controlled, healthy, and positive manners.

If your child has a gift, a belief, or an interest in maintaining spirit contact, learn as much as you can about spirit guides and ancestor veneration. There are hundreds of books on this particular subject; you can surf the net, check out the New Age or Metaphysical section in bookstores, or go to the nearest library. And the biggest help of all is seeking out and talking to people who may be familiar or experienced with your particular situation. You may be surprised that you are not alone and that many others can relate to your experience—believe me, I know firsthand. There are also licensed counselors and therapists who incorporate spiritualism into their methods of healing. Most importantly, know that you do not need to commit to or feel obligated to any entity or person—just inquire and learn. Whatever you do, the knowledge gained, if handled carefully, might very well lead you and your family to a much happier and spiritually rewarding life.

Please know that I have explained this information with the best intentions. But no matter how positive or true *my* intentions, I must not neglect to mention that there are loopholes when dealing with the spirit world. There are people, families, and groups with false intentions. They will even go as far as sending bad spirits to other people for evil and unnecessary reasons. What really makes this kind of situation bad is that these individuals don't realize that when they send negative energy to a person, that energy does not necessarily hit the intended person. It can hit their children instead, and in return, the affects on the children are damaging in vast ways.

These people live very unclean and negative lives; therefore, they attract similar spirits. If you are a person with malice in your heart, then you will attract human company and spirits of the same. If you are a person who causes trouble and likes confusion, then this is the energy that you will attract. Therefore, stringent care must be taken when dealing with the spirit world. This is why positive thinking and a positive way of life are very important. Spirits are attracted to our deeds and vibrations, and many times they will feed off of our emotions. You must know and be clear about your intentions when dealing with the invisible world—the good attracts good, and the bad will attract bad. I hope that this information has brought you clarity and will be beneficial to you and your entire family.

CHAPTER 7

SPIRIT STORIES

One can only imagine my many encounters during the years that I have been dealing with the spirits. The following stories and experiences, collected from my own experiences and those of my family and closest friends, are from spirit guides on the other side. They will give you an idea about how different the "personalities" are from spirit to spirit, and will also show you the various ways that guides can communicate and help us during our lives.

The following message was received during a very moving séance that my godmother gave several years ago. A special request made by one of her ancestors brought tears to my eyes. The request was that we pray for all spirits that were slaves. The spirit making the request, female and with an older appearance, was very upset and scolded us for forgetting them, for failing to recognize their contributions, and for taking for granted the many "rights" that they suffered, fought, and died for over the centuries. She communicated that she felt very hurt by the fact that we do not even think about them. I felt bad because this was so sad, yet true. How many of us pray for all those who have walked before us? How many of us, on a regular basis, think about those who endured suffering, beatings, and death so that we would have the "right" to be educated, have equal rights, vote, end oppression, etc.? How many of us pray and ask for the guidance and insight of our ancestors who were slaves? We continue to fight for the same issues that they faced, and we are still fighting to know and embrace our true heritage.

The funny thing is, I felt I had received a wake-up call and recollected how the only time I may have thought about our enslaved ancestors was probably Black History Month. I was guilty of all the things the spirit mentioned, and I will never forget that very moving moment. Because of this important special request, I ask that everyone who reads this keep conscious thoughts and prayers focused on all our ancestors, especially the ones who were enslaved, so that they may guide our steps and help us fight our battles as we continue to fight towards freedom and equality throughout human existence.

This story is from my daughter, who can and does communicate with her guides on occasion. For a long time, she was aware of only one particular spirit who was constantly around, named Chola. I had the rare opportunity to get this very important story, which I am retelling in my own words.

Chola is a fun-loving spirit, sometimes too fun-loving. She's sexy and wild. She states that she has been reincarnated at least three times, once as a cat. The other two times she lived short lives because she was hardheaded. Both times she died early (in her mid-thirties) because she never wanted to listen. She thought she knew it all. Chola had no respect for authority— she thought she could do whatever she wanted to do. (My theory is that since Chola had a previous life as a cat, an animal that is usually free to roam, human life was difficult for her, because animals do not have to deal with human issues. If she was a "street" cat that could explain her wildness.)

During her first human life, Chola was coming from the grocery store and not paying attention while crossing the street, and she was hit by a car. Paralyzed from the waist down and in a wheelchair, she died several months later when she wheeled her chair backwards out of her room and accidentally rolled down a flight of stairs. Upon receiving a second chance (a new incarnation), she went through life just as hardheaded as the first time. She states that her second death occurred while walking past a building under construction—a brick fell on top of her head and split it. After being operated on, she died after being in a coma for three weeks.

Now she has the challenge and assignment of living and learning life's lessons through my daughter.

Chola states that she now understands why God ended her life early, twice. She says that she does not want my daughter to go through life the way she did. She also states that she is the little birdie that whispers in my ear and tells on my daughter when she sees that my daughter is about to do something she has no business doing.

As a spirit, Chola was not always this way. She was just as hardheaded and stubborn as before, and at times disrespectful, but with spiritual work, communication, and prayer, she has learned— and is still learning—to see the light. She now realizes that her responsibility is for someone other than herself. We still have a ways to go, but she's growing as my daughter grows, and if she truly wants to elevate, she will meet her challenges head on so that she can finally evolve.

As you can only imagine, this story is very important to me because my daughter must now learn the lessons that were not learned by the spirit of Chola, and hopefully my daughter will pass her tests of this life so that I do not have to lose a daughter at an early age.

While my daughter and I were talking one day, she said she felt disappointed that I had many spirits around me and that she had only one. I told her that she had more, but it was not their time to reveal themselves. A few weeks later, she was jumping for joy because another spirit had revealed itself and offered the perfect opportunity to get this story.

Luli is a spirit from the Afrikan continent and is the total opposite of Chola. She's book smart and a loner. As far as she remembers, she only lived one lifetime. Luli died at the ripe old age of 110, and she credits happiness for her longevity; I pray that I am blessed to live as long as she did. During her life, she lived in Nigeria, where she learned the mysteries of vodou.

One day, she was at the spiritual market buying her usual oils, powders, and potions. With her hands full and not watching where she was walking, she bumped into a man and dropped all her supplies. He proceeded to help her pick up her things and they began to talk. They were instantly attracted to each other. One thing led to another, and after six months of courtship, they decided to live together. After one year, they got married. Sadly, they never had any children. Luli loved him so much that she tattooed her arm with a red rose and Nigerian words that would translate to something similar to, "Til death do us part."

During the first couple of years of their marriage, she suspected her husband of cheating on her. She eventually found out that he was having intimate relations with another woman. She felt hurt and betrayed, but she decided that her love was strong enough for her to stick it out. Separation was not negotiable. After some time, he came to his senses and both of them came to terms with their love for each other. She never revealed if her mysteries had anything to do with it, but she said that their remaining years together were happy ones, even though she never fully trusted him. He lived to be 90, and his death was the beginning of her unhappiness. Luli eventually died at 110, and once in the afterlife, she did get to see her beloved. They remained friends up until it was time for them to go their separate ways in the spirit realm. She said that the lesson she wanted to share with us is that relationships will have their pains and disappointments, but with love and the grace of God you really can hold it all together.

Since meeting Luli, my daughter has been introduced to several others spirit guides, but Chola and Luli are my favorites, so far.

As for me, most of my guides speak to me in dreams. I will share one of my dream stories with you. Our guides can show us serious dreams, happy dreams, not-so-happy dreams, or what I call "nosey" dreams. Nosey dreams are dreams of little significance about other people's lives. For example:

One night I had a dream about my job, where two people, a boss and his secretary, were having sexual relations. I didn't know these people, both in my dream and in real life. They could have been anybody. I went to work the next day and I told one of my closest friends about the dream. I usually tell someone close about my dreams so that when they come true I will have a witness. Sure enough, two months later the whole office was buzzing about a president and his assistant having sexual relations.

I gathered two things from my dream: (1) the guides gave me a vague dream because if they had shown me exactly who the two people were, I would have spoken about the dream and revealed the identity of the people before it was time for other people to know, and (2) the dream gave me more confidence in the existence of my guides because they showed me something that did come true, even in its vaguest form.

Many times we do not realize that the spirits will not reveal information to us before it is time, because they know that as humans we tend to get carried away with our emotions and we act hastily upon things that may lead us into trouble, no matter how minor. Imagine if the spirits had shown me exactly who the two parties were. I would have revealed this information innocently, not to gossip but to have a witness validate my dream. Now imagine the information seeping out, and these two people finding out that the information started with me—they would probably have made my life hell at work. I am saying all of this to show that many times the spirits will give us vague information so that we cannot cause innocent or intentional harm to others or ourselves.

We tend to think that our guides are around us all the time, but they aren't. A common belief is that throughout our lives we all have at least one guardian with us the whole time, along with other guides who remain until their moment of elevation occurs or a particular task is accomplished. But on a daily basis, our guides come and go. This brings us to a situation I found myself in when trying to call one of my guides for something she thought was trivial.

I have a female guide who I call Nana. At times, she can have a nasty attitude because she dislikes being bothered. You can equate her to a cranky old lady—she's no-nonsense. She's the type of spirit that only likes to be called when absolutely necessary, but she's excellent at solving issues, and if you ask her a question, you can bet your last dollar that she will give you a 98 percent accurate answer. She calls it like she sees it. Despite her demeanor, I am very close to her, and I talk to her a lot. One day I was in one of those weird, lonesome moods, and I just wanted to feel her presence around, so I called upon her. I usually can feel when she's around, but this time I felt nothing, so I continued to call. At first, I was wondering if she had heard me. Then I was wondering what she possibly could be doing that was taking her so long to come (like she has nothing else to do). Finally, she sent a message through one of my daughter's guides, and the message was, "I know you don't want nothin', child, and I am on vacation. There's nothing going on in your life right now that you need me for, so call me next week!" I was thoroughly amused and shocked at the same time. It never occurred to me that spirits take breaks, too. I was tickled by the fact that she'd heard me calling her, but she was not about to break her vacation because I wanted "nothing." This is when I realized that our guides do not just sit around watching us all day, and they do not jump to answer our every beck and call. They come when we have a legitimate need for help.

Sometimes I used to wonder if the same ancestors who guide me also guide other people in my family, and then I had this dream:

My Native Amerikan ancestors revealed that they work together as a tribe—men, women, and children. In the dream, they revealed that different members of this tribe help at different times and for different situations in my life. They also showed me that some of them help other people in my family on different levels but will work collectively, splitting duties for the total interest of the family. Then there are some family members who do not need the help of the Indians because they have other ancestors to help them instead. I know this is true with my daughter and a first cousin of mine. My daughter has ancestors from her father's side of the family who primarily help her. My first cousin has seen a Native Amerikan ancestor from the same tribe as mine who helps her, which led me to believe that we share the same tribe.

The following is an experience and story contributed from my godsister about a "Spirit in White." This is a factual account of my encounter with a spirit that my godfather told me would definitely happen. During a reading, he said, "Something is going to come in your door, good or bad, but something is going to come through your front door." I was not expecting to actually see or hear it. I just figured it would be an actual person or something invisible that I would not notice.

At any rate, the story begins with me wanting a break from my three kids. I sent them to visit their great-grandmother for the weekend. The kids were gone, and I was home alone on a Saturday night relaxing, for a change, in a quiet house. I decided to do some cleaning, and I put my Walkman on so I would not disturb my neighbors. With music in my ears, I got into a really intense cleaning mode. At about 9:15 p.m., I went to the sink to wash the dishes. After about ten minutes or so, I was bobbing my head to the tunes and I was in the groove, and suddenly I heard my front door open. Even with the Walkman on, I could hear the squeaky door open. I thought to myself, "Why would my grandmother send the boys home so late without calling first?" Then I thought to myself, "She wouldn't do that." Then, two seconds later, I thought the worst: "My God—someone is coming into my house." I panicked and grabbed a kitchen knife just in case. When I turned to my right, I was literally frozen with shock, fear, and surprise when I saw the most amazing thing I have ever seen in my entire life.

She was tall and floating about two inches off the ground, more graceful than any ballerina anyone has ever laid eyes upon. She was almost transparent, yet not quite. She had on a pure white gown, whiter than white. It was very beautiful, with a long, floor-length, flowing skirt. She walked right down my hallway and into the living room. She looked at me, I looked at her, and she disappeared. My jaw was wide open, and I did everything from pinching myself to talking out loud, just to prove that I was awake and that I had actually seen her.

I looked around the living room. It was calm and cool. I stood in the spot where she had been when she vanished and looked around some more. I went to the front door and nothing was amiss or out of place, but I know I heard my front door open and close the same way it always did. I knew I wasn't losing my mind, but my next thought was, "Am I?" I rushed to call my godfather to tell

*him what I had just witnessed, and he was thrilled. He said that it
was a very good thing. Then he asked if I was sure she was in
white, and I replied that I could not be any surer. He said, "We've
got to make sure she does not leave you. That is an Obàtálá." That
is a great blessing, and he laughed when I said she walked right in
the front door, just like he said she would. Maferefun!*

From that day on, everyone in my house has had an
encounter with this spirit. One night, my middle son got up
to use the bathroom, as children often do in the middle of
the night, and I heard a scream. I jumped out of bed to see
my son looking like he'd just seen a ghost. He had. He said
someone in a white robe scurried past him really fast when
he turned on the light in the bathroom. I explained to him
what it was, and he was cool from then on. For us, these
occurrences are so frequent they have become the norm.
And because my oldest son also sees spirits on a regular
basis, my middle son has gotten used to hearing such stories
and having those experiences.

On another occasion, a few months later, a friend was
visiting. While sitting in the living room, my friend said to
me, "There is someone in here with a white robe or dress
on," and I had to laugh, as I knew my spirit was just letting
us all know she was still there. My friend also said the
person was very, very light, and I know she meant that my
spirit was surrounded in light, as I had seen her once before.
Over time, my friends have realized that they will encounter
unique experiences one way or another when visiting my
home. Lately, I do not see her (the spirit in white) as often as
I used to; she used to be out and about every other day, it
seemed. My family, friends, and I would hear someone
walking around the apartment night and day when we were
in bed or in different rooms, or there would be constant
activity in the living room where I had my ancestral altar
(boveda or vovoda) set up. And now that I'm living in a

different apartment, I have only seen her two or three times in the past year. But I am sure she's still with me, and for that I am happy.

A dear friend of mine, L. Davis, contributed the following story:

I was introduced to Santeria at a very early age; however, at that age, I never knew the name for it. I remember my mom praying to saint-like images in our home, but the ones you don't normally see in Catholic churches like St. Elias. The statues I remember most were a Black saint and an American Indian statue that stood at the front door with a glass of water. These were things I considered to be normal, but I never knew the true meaning behind them. I remember so many different spiritual or supernatural encounters I had, some of which I wouldn't have believed if they hadn't happened to me, personally. There's one experience I had as a child that is very similar to the movie The Exorcist. I was six years old when I was possessed by some kind of entity. I remember being told how my parents had to break down my bedroom door because they couldn't get in when I was crying for them. My bed was shaking terribly, and I had some kind of unseen force field around me where my parents couldn't touch me. Something or someone was pushing them away each time they attempted to grab me. My brothers and sister were crying because they couldn't understand what was happening, and my mother began reading from the Bible and praying while throwing holy water on me. The bed began slowing down, but it wouldn't stop. My mother ran to her room and made a phone call to a well-known spiritualist/santero in our town of New Brunswick, New Jersey. This man arrived in our home to find me still lying down on this bed that was clearly still moving, and I was told that he asked my parents to leave the room as he began the exorcism.

I don't recall how long it took him to cast this thing away, but my parents were allowed back in the room to comfort me. I was told he continued blessing the home and stabbing or cutting each room with a knife. I was never told the specific reason for this, but it's been twenty-five years later, and I still have this "spiritual knife" secretly hidden away. My parents were told never to throw it away, and they kept it all these years until I bought my first home, when it was then given to me.

This santero told my parents that I was blessed with spiritual gifts and that good and evil forces would constantly fight over me, so it was very important to keep a close eye on me. About a week later, our family was notified that this man died while in his sleep. No one knew the true reason behind his death, but my mom assumes to this day that my event had something to do with it. Needless to say, that was the first of many spiritual experiences I had.

CHAPTER 8

RITUAL SUCCESS AND DEVELOPMENT

What is meant by ritual? Basically, a ritual is a customary, repeated act, but a ritual can also be a ceremony, a sacrament, or a formal procedure. For this book, we are mostly dealing with the second part of the definition and referring to a ritual as a ceremony, specifically for the use of working magic and working with your ancestors and spirit guides/eguns.

As in most spiritual systems, the main ingredients to any successful ritual are *positive attitude and good intentions.* There are so many different spiritual traditions that, when it comes to rituals or performing any kind of magic work, different people do different things. The motto is, "Whatever works." What may work for one person may not necessarily work for another. Many people give up when they feel that a ritual is not working. Time, patience, and persistence are the makings of a successful ritual. With study, exploration, and practice you will gain knowledge that will help you build a solid foundation for your spiritual development. The following are just a few suggestions for preparing yourself for a ritual.

Clean your house or space—get your living area in order and remove whatever you don't want or need. Throw away anything that needs to be in the garbage. Get rid of clutter, especially in the corners, closets, and under beds, because this attracts negative vibrations. Some people love storing things in plastic bags, but plastic bags collect unwanted energies. Get rid of them and organize your items in boxes or plastic storage bins. Once done, you may choose to spiritually cleanse your work area or your home with a floor wash or herbal mixture, and burn some sort of purifying incense to cleanse and lift the vibration levels (the air) of your living space or workspace. You can expect better results when you remove negative energies to attract positive ones.

The next thing you may want to do is create sacred space. This can be an altar or shrine (sometimes called a white table or boveda/vovoda) for your ancestors or spirit guides/eguns on a small table, a dresser top, or the floor. A floor shrine is set in the corner of a room, usually the basement, kitchen, or bathroom. When setting your altar/shrine, you may want to include pictures of your deceased relatives or items that belong to them. Your altar/shrine can be as fancy, moderate, or simple as you would like it to be. However or wherever you decide to create your altar/shrine, it should be in an uninterrupted place—a sacred place, where you are sure no one will bother it. Although setting an altar or shrine is optional, it is beneficial not just for spirit but to those who may have a hard time focusing, concentrating, or working with spirit with just the mind. The altar or shrine becomes the focal point or rendezvous place where you maintain a relationship with God and those who have departed.

The basic altar should include at least one large glass of water, a candle (preferably white), flowers (preferably white), a cross or a symbol that is sacred to you, like the Star of David, and a Bible, prayer book, or writings of inspiration. One of the reasons for using white and setting your altar with the indicated items is to set the mood for a very pleasant and uplifting environment that will attract intelligent, good, and superior spirits. Remember, the color white is very cool and calming, and the vibration of the color white signifies purity and truth. Other colors can throw off the mood and will attract other energies that you may not be ready to handle. There are many variations on how an altar/shrine is created, depending on the individual, the level of expertise, or the culture. In many instances, people will have one altar specifically designated for their ancestors (family members) and a separate shrine located in a totally different location designated for all the other spirit guides. For example, many people in my culture have spirit/egun

shrines set in special corners of their homes, preferably in the basement, kitchen, or bathroom. At a minimum, these floor shrines will include a consecrated spirit/egun staff, dressed with ribbons and bells, used for calling the spirits, a glass of water, a small glass of rum, a cup of coffee, a cigar or cigarette, and a bouquet of flowers. Additional offerings are usually given on special occasions or when special requests are made. *(See caring for your Altar)*

Note: If you are a novice at spiritual communication, use only one glass of water and one candle on your altar or shrine in your initial stages, according to recommendations. For the beginner, simple is always better. And when placing that glass of water and candle upon your altar/shrine, dedicate them to God and your guardian angel and spirit protectors so that you do not attract any unwanted spirits that may be hanging around at the time. Many spirits need and want light and prayer, and they will try to get it any way they can. In some cases there is nothing wrong with this, except you could be attracting unclean spirit energy. For obvious reasons, this is not a good thing when you are trying to make and maintain direct communication with your own personal guardian spirits.

For those of you who are familiar with spirit communication and already have altars or shrines set, you may use three, five, seven, or nine glasses of water. When people do this, it is often because they have seen or read that they must. While this is typically okay, it may not be good for everyone. Remember, what works for one person may not necessarily work for another. However, if your spiritual teacher (elder) or your spirit guides reveal that a specific number of glasses should be used, then by all means use them. But if your elder or guide has not communicated such information, yet you are experimenting with it, you are in the position of possibly attracting unwanted and mischievous spirits that can be lingering around your home or workplace. If you choose to use more than one glass of water, each glass should be specifically dedicated to a spirit guide or group of guides as they reveal themselves to you. For instance, I have at least five primary spirit guides that I work with, plus my ancestors. So I place and dedicate one glass of water to all my ancestors except for my deceased brother, who has specifically requested his own glass. Then I have one glass for my madama, one for the Indians, one for the Afrikans, one for the gypsies, and one for other guides that walk with me. So I use seven glasses, but if another guide comes forward I will add an additional glass, which would then add up to eight.

A variation is to take seven glasses of water and place a cross on the top of one glass, which should be dedicated to God. Create a circle around this one glass with the other six. Those six glasses will be generically dedicated to different groups of spirits. For instance, one glass will be dedicated to the American Indians, one to the Afrikans, one to the spirits of Asian descent, one to the madamas or slaves, one to the gypsies, and one to all your ancestors. This is a pretty standard method for those in the Santeria or Lukumi communities to recommend to individuals who do not know the types of spirits they have in their spiritual tribe/domain.

In some systems, specific reasons determine the number of glasses of water used and the strategic placement of the glasses upon the altars/shrines in circles or in the shape of a "V." For instance, in some cultures seven glasses of water are placed to specially appease and gain aid from the spirit realm to help only family members, or in some instances, nine glasses of water are placed to specially invoke the Afrikan spirits. Other variations include placing the glasses in a circle to gain success, or lining them up in a "V" for defense.

When dealing with the realm of spirit, the variations of how altars can be set and how they can be used are endless. Within various cultures and spiritual systems, there are usually a few standard rules to follow; however, spiritualism is vast, and every individual can and will do different things when it comes to the spirit world. It is not my intention to say what is right and what is wrong. My true intention is safety. I just want you to know how to be careful, to be aware, and to question how to deal with the spirit world. I do not want you to bring unnecessary harm unto yourself by giving or exchanging energy and light with unwanted, mischievous, and dangerous spirits that do not belong to you. Learn how to be aware of what you are dealing with so that the correct decisions can be made and the correct actions can be taken.

Once you have prepared your area and your altar/shrine, you will want to start a dialogue and begin a relationship with your ancestors or spirit guides. When beginning to communicate with your guides, set aside a day and time when you will be able to pray or talk to them, uninterrupted. When ready, I recommend beginning your communication with prayer, for example, the Lord's Prayer, the Twenty-third Psalm, any guardian angel prayers, any prayers of light, or poems of inspiration. Prayers in general will establish communications of love, health, positivism, and goodness. And if there are any bad spirits lurking close by, this will let them know that their communication or assistance is unwanted and that you will not tolerate or leave yourself open to any negative or evil thought forms. After prayer, you can feel free to talk, cry, or laugh with your guides like you would with a friend. Do whatever makes you comfortable! Sometimes I find myself actually praying to them and sometimes I'm talking to them as I would with a friend sitting right next to me. It will all depend on your mood. It is just that easy. Many of you, without realizing it, have already experienced spirit contact on some level or another, but because of lack of knowledge and/or conscious/subconscious fear, you have chosen to ignore it or have refused to recognize it for what it is. After some time (it can be days or weeks) of communing with your spirit guides, you may see, feel, or hear a counter-response from your guides. Your ancestors or guides will also give you messages or reveal themselves through your dreams, so pay close attention. Dreams are the easiest way for spirits to communicate with us, because sleeping is when we are the most relaxed. If possible, keep a dream journal so that you can write down your dreams as soon as you wake up. This will help you strengthen your dream recall.

As the relationship between you and your spirit guides becomes stronger and they come closer to you, you may begin to feel different. The results will vary from person to person. Some of you will feel nauseated or get headaches when you feel spirit energy. Others will feel big and strong or weak and fragile. Some of you may feel heat or cool air around you, and others may feel sensations on different parts of your body, like someone is playing in your hair or the hairs are going up on the back of your neck and on your arms. Sometimes you can actually feel your guides standing behind or next to you, or you may even feel them sit on the bed next to you. Other signs from your ancestors or guides may include a sudden flood of emotions like laughing or crying; a flow of messages in your mind; or the urge to buy things—like statues that might represent the ancestors or guides or do things that they once did—and you will not know why. You may even get the desire to take a smoke or a drink of their favorite liquor, or you may develop sensitivity to the smells of perfumes and flowers. These are just some examples of how your guides may be letting you know that they are around and listening to you. If you see, feel, or hear things that make you uncomfortable, remember that you are in control, and you do not have to be afraid to rebuke or pray away any negative or unwanted spirit energy.

You may also prepare and work your rituals and spirit guides for other people, but beware. Negativity and harmful intentions will not go far. Many people fail to realize that harmful magic or misuse of the spirit guides **can and will backfire**. There are several reasons for this: (1) your own spirit guides can get angry and punish you themselves; (2) your target (the other person) will have his or her own protective guides that may retaliate and reverse everything back towards you; (3) universal justice or divine intervention—what goes around, comes around; and (4) your target may find out and get you back. The bottom line is, if you do bad or evil, you will get it back when you least expect it, in most cases with little or no sympathy. So be careful about what you do to others. "We live in the hell that we create for others. No one can elude justice. Reparations can be delayed, but they are inevitable."[10]

Keeping that in mind, when you do spiritual work for yourself or others, adequately cleanse and protect yourself so you do not pick up unwanted and unknown vibrations and energies from the person or situation you are working with. You should frequently take spiritual baths as added protection. For example, you can pick up an illness or get sick from headaches and nausea, or sometimes a bad entity can attach itself to you, and the next thing you know, you find yourself with problems and issues that do not belong to you. Do not work with or help others unless you are very experienced or confident that you can handle the matter. If you are thinking about doing spiritual work for someone else, know that it is best to seek out an elder or a more experienced individual who is skilled in this area.

All in all, be very clear about your intentions when speaking to spirits or when doing magic, especially in rituals pertaining to love or in rituals where there is a need to defend or protect yourself. These are the two primary areas where people tend to get overemotional. In the area of love, many times people cross the line from a simple attraction ritual to a ritual of domination against an individual's own will. It is one thing to prepare rituals to appear more appealing and attractive to someone or to give that special person a harmless push towards you, but it is a totally different matter when you try and force the issue against that person's will and spirit for your own selfish gain. This is considered the darker side of magic, which in the end will wind up getting you hurt. Another hard area to control is the area of defense or retaliation when situations and people anger you. When you are under high emotional stress or upset, you really need to be careful and aware of what kind of energy you are projecting or magic you are doing. The energy that you radiate and the words that you speak are usually hot and can easily be absorbed into your ritual. Because of this, you can really hurt someone, even unintentionally. You can also aim your magic and accidentally hit the wrong person, because hot energy—angry energy—is usually erratic. So as a warning, fully think through your process, whether for good or bad, before working your magic, because even innocent magic can hurt.

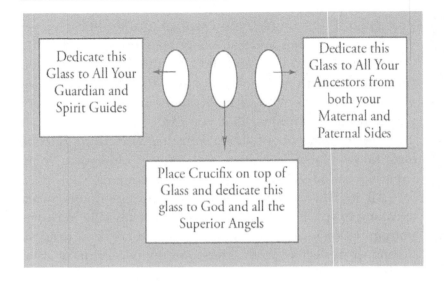

BASIC ALTAR

THREE GLASSES OF WATER SETUP

Assuming that your home is now clean of all clutter and debris and has been swept and mopped, you are ready to prepare your altar. Before preparing your altar, incense your home entirely with purifying incense, such as white sage, frankincense, sandalwood, or copal—especially in the room and around the space where the altar will be set.

ITEMS FOR BASIC ALTAR

- 3 clear glasses
- 1 vase for flowers
- 1 bouquet of white flowers
- 1 cross or crucifix with or without Jesus hanging on it (Some cultures do not use the crucifix with Jesus hanging on it, and this is fine. They would use the cross with no image on it; for many, the cross actually represents the four directions of the world.)
- 1 Bible, Qur'an, Torah, book of inspirational prayers,

or whatever sacred book that was the faith of your
ancestors
- Pictures of your deceased relatives, if you have any
- 1 seven-day white candle, tea light, or stick candle
- Holy water
- Florida water, Kolonia 1800, or any fragrance of your
  choice, such as rose water, lavender water, orange
  water, etc.
- Incense—preferably white sage, frankincense,
  sandalwood, or copal
- Self-igniting charcoal
- Rum
- Cigars
- Cascarilla/Efun
- Ancestral staff/stick—see next section for preparation
  instructions

PREPARATION OF ALTAR

Fill a medium-sized bowl halfway with plain tap water
and mix in a little holy water, Florida water, or fragrance of
your choice, and rum. Light a cigar and blow a lot of smoke
over the mixture. While mixing, pray:

*In the name of all that is holy, just, and pure in light, love,
truth, and wisdom, let this mixture be blessed and purified for my
intended purpose. I call upon my guardian angel and superior
guides to give me the strength and the energy to charge these
ingredients with love, positivity, and nothing but goodness so that
all negativity and evil influences will be turned away and removed
from this space that is being cleansed for the purpose of
communicating with my ancestors and spirit guides.*

When done, save a little of the blessed mixture to wash
and wipe down some of the items that you have. With the

rest of the mixture, wipe down the entire table, dresser, or shelving that you have chosen to use as your altar, all the while praying to your ancestors and your guardian spirits for help and light with your intentions for the setup of this altar.

1. Place a clean white cloth on the surface of your altar.
2. Place pictures of your deceased relatives on the altar, toward the back.
3. Take the three glasses and wash them out with the mixture that you made in the bowl. Rinse the glasses with tap water, then fill them with water until it's 1/4 inch from the brim. Place the glasses on the altar as shown in the illustration.
4. Place the cross or crucifix on top of the middle glass, for this glass is dedicated to God and the superior spirits.
5. Place the vase with flowers behind the middle glass of water towards the back of your altar, but in front of the pictures.
6. Place the seven-day candle in front of the middle glass. For safety, place the candle in water in a candleholder, can, bowl, or something else that can hold water. You can also burn a tea light in a saucer with water.
7. Place the Bible, Qur'an, Torah, or inspirational book on the left side of your altar.
8. Place any belongings of your deceased relatives anyplace on the altar, preferably near their pictures, providing you have space.
9. Place the additional items such as the holy water, fragranced water, cigars, and rum on the altar on the right-hand side near the front for easy access when you need them.

These instructions for your altar are for a basic setup.

You can create your altar any way you like and in any way that makes you comfortable. Altars can be made on floors, tables, dresser tops, bookcases, or shelves on walls. Placement of your altar will depend on your space, and in this case, you will improvise as necessary. You may not have room to place all the desired items, and that's okay. If your space allows for only one glass of water and a candle, then that's what you should use. Don't worry if things are not perfect. The most ancestors and/or spirit guides. Now that your altar is set, you can begin your communications with your ancestors.

PREPARATION OF ANCESTRAL STAFF

There are many ways that you can prepare an ancestral or spirit/egun staff, especially if you have a relationship with a priest or priestess who is familiar with this process. A staff consecrated by a priest is a ceremonial staff called an opa iku. The opa iku is a summoning stick used to call the ancestors and/or spirits to your aid. Typically, an opa iku should, but does not have to, have a snake carved on it. The purpose of the carved snake (if consecrated properly) is to represent the spiral of life and how a baby comes into the world and spirals in its mother's womb. When a person uses this stick, the spirits that are summoned spiral into this world from the other dimensions. They spiral up and around the stick like a snake and into the hand of the person who holds its power. Different spirits enter into our world through different methods—some through water, mirrors, or doors. Think of the opa iku as a portal that some spirits need to visit the person for whom the opa iku has been divined. Divination is necessary because an opa iku is not for everyone, and these staffs are tailor-made to an individual per the instructions of the spirit realm through the divination process. These staffs are consecrated with specific prayers, rituals, and sacrifices. Because of this, the opa iku holds more power than ancestral staffs.

If you know of or have a relationship with an initiated priest who can consecrate this staff for you, great. If not, simple instructions follow regarding how you can prepare and bless your own staff, which is not to be confused with an opa iku. The difference is that anyone can have and make their own spiritual staff or summoning stick, but an opa iku is only given when specifically asked for by the person's ancestors or spirit guides and is consecrated by a priest or priestess.

ITEMS FOR PREPARATION

- A tree branch or stick from outdoors that is at least 3 feet tall and 2 1/2 inches in diameter. Make sure the stick is as straight as possible.
- 9 different colored pieces of ribbon, each at least 12 to 15 inches long
- 9 bells
- 1 tea light, with extras handy (If one goes out, light another.)
- 1 saucer
- Holy water
- Florida water
- Plain tap water
- Palm Oil/Manteca de Corojo
- Cascarilla/Egg Shell Powder/Efun
- Cigar
- Honey
- Sharp knife
- An empty pail

1. Place newspaper on the floor and use a knife to carve all the bark off the branch/stick. As you are working

to prepare your ancestral staff, pray during each step, letting your ancestors and spirit guides know that you are preparing this staff because it will be used to call forth their presence. Pray that you want nothing but positive energies flowing through your ancestral staff, etc.

2. Once all the bark has been carved off, clean up all the carvings and throw them away with the newspaper.

3. Firmly tie each ribbon onto your branch/staff, leaving some of each piece of ribbon hanging to tie the bells to.

4. Tie the bells onto the ribbons, one bell per ribbon.

5. Place an empty pail on the floor. You may want to place newspaper or an old towel underneath the pail to absorb any wetness that may occur from the following.

6. Take the saucer and pour some water onto it. Light a tea light, place it on the saucer with water, and put it right in front of the pail on the floor. The water is for fire safety and to protect the saucer from becoming too hot from the tea light.

7. Take tap water and pour it all over the branch/stick, from top to bottom. With your hands, rub the branch/stick, ribbons, and stick, including the front, back, sides, top, and bottom. During each of the following steps, you will continue to pray and repeat your intentions for this staff as in step 1.

8. Pour holy water all over the branch/stick, ribbons, and bells, and continue as in step 7.

9. Pour Florida water all over the branch/stick, ribbons, and bells, and continue as in step 7.

10. Pour or put palm oil into your hands, and rub them all over the branch/stick, ribbons, and bells, the same as in step 7.

11. Crumble carcarilla/eggshell powder into your hands

and rub it all over the branch/stick, ribbons, and bells, the same as in step 7.

12. Pour a little honey into your hands and rub it all over the branch/stick, ribbons, and bells, the same as in step 7.

13. When you are all done, wash your hands. Light your cigar and puff on it, filling your mouth with smoke (do not inhale). Blow the smoke out onto your branch/stick, ribbons, and bells. Do this at least three times.

14. Now take a mouthful of rum (do not swallow) and blow the rum out of your mouth onto the branch/stick. Do this at least three times. If you find it difficult to blow the rum out of your mouth, pour the rum directly onto the branch/stick, rubbing it all over.

The staff is now complete. Take your ancestral staff and lean it up against your altar. Clean up everything, and if your candle is still burning, place it on the floor in front of your staff.

Each time that you decide to go to your altar and pray, take your staff in your left hand (your power hand), lift it, and tap the floor while calling your ancestors' names and while praying.

For instance, you will pray:

As I sit/stand in front of my altar, I call upon the spirits of my ancestors. I call upon my ancestors from near and from far. I call upon my distant ancestors and those recently deceased. I call upon all those I know and remember and all those I have forgotten but whose blood runs through my veins. Greetings and good blessings to: [say the name of one of your ancestors, tap your staff on the floor, say another name of one of your ancestors, tap your staff on the floor, say another name of one of your ancestors, tap your staff on the floor, and continue until all names have been said].

After you have finished saying the names of all the ancestors that you can remember, you will continue to tap your staff while saying:

I've come to ask for your continued blessings and for you to hear my prayers. Ancestors, I ask that you walk before me so I can avoid straying and being lost. Walk before me as my guide around the pitfalls and traps of my enemies. Walk before me as a beacon of light so that I may never know darkness. Walk before me so that I may follow your example of pride and humility. Walk before me with patience, for I may not always be able to keep up.

Ancestors, I welcome your communications and I ask that you help my family and me with all our daily difficulties. I ask that you help me remove my obstacles with minimal pain and suffering. I welcome your guidance and instruction with all sincerity, and I promise my best to learn your teachings and to heed your warnings. Ancestors, there's no love like family love, and I ask that you continue loving and protecting me, keeping me safe and peaceful always.

With blessings from the Supreme Being and in the name of all that is holy, just, pure in light, love, truth, and wisdom, I will pray for you always. Amen.

This is just an example of a prayer that you could say. After you have finished saying it or something similar, you can place your staff back in its original place. From this point, you can continue saying whatever prayers or requests you have in mind. The staff is used as a traditional method for calling the spirits; it is a tool for gaining the attention of your ancestors and/or spirit guides. Other methods for calling the spirits include the use of bells and/or rattlers, for this is how some spirits prefer to be called.

Caring for Your Altar

1. Your altar should be cleaned at least once a week, or whatever your schedule permits. Glasses of water should be washed, cleaned, and refilled at least once a week as well.

2. As your schedule permits, give your ancestors coffee or tea, a shot glass of rum, a small glass of wine, or a different drink. Liquors do not always have to be rum; you can place gin, brandy, or whatever was their favorite.

   You may also give your ancestors cooked foods. Ideally, you should prepare the foods that your ancestors would have eaten in their time, but it is acceptable to give them foods that you cook for yourself and your family. You can do this once a week or once a month, depending on which spiritual system you decide to follow. Some spiritual systems will have you feed the ancestors as needed, with no set timing. But when you do feed your ancestors, serve them the first plate. You can serve them full portions of food on an adult-sized plate or smaller portions on a tea-sized saucer. You can put out fruits, sweets, sandwiches, candies, crackers, a piece of bread, or other foods. If you need to remove the foods before the week is out because of odor or bugs, this is okay. It is very acceptable to leave the foods for one day and then discard them the next day. If food offerings are a part of an ebbo, the spirit may ask that the food be discarded somewhere other than the garbage, such as a crossroads (two streets or roads that cross each other in the form of a "t") or a park.

   It is also acceptable to give large offerings of food, drink, and sweets only when asking for a favor.

You do not want to spoil your ancestors. They are here to help you no matter what. Some people are under the misconception that the more they give their ancestors, the more their ancestors will give them. This is not true. Sometimes our ancestors will get lazy. The relationship should be a fair and reasonable exchange.

3. Offerings to the spirits can include anything from foods, including fruits or sweets, to flowers to toys. If you are working with a departed loved one, you can make their favorite meal as a special offering in exchange for their assistance. A priest/priestess can prescribe offerings, or you can go by your own intuition. Whatever you give, give from your heart. When you make a promise to your guides, make sure that you fulfill it. If you promise flowers, candies, or candles, give the promised item(s) when you say that you will, for some spirits tend not to be particularly forgiving.

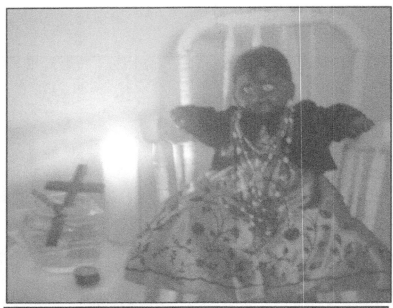

THE VOICE OF TRUTH
by Ernest Holmes

The Voice of Truth speaks to me and through me.

The Voice of Truth guides me and keeps me on the path of the perfect day.

I will listen to the Inner Voice and It will tell me what to do in the hour of need.

I shall be told everything that I ought to know when the time of need arrives, and I shall not be misled.

The Voice of Truth cannot lie, but always speaks to me from On High.

Nothing enters but this Voice, for it is the Voice of God.

God speaks to me.

CHAPTER 9

TOOLS OF THE TRADE

As with any kind of work, tools and preparations are needed to ensure success of your rituals. A few simple guidelines appear below. I have followed these steps over the years because they worked for me. You can choose to either use them or not use them. They are also provided for those who prefer using a more organized system. Other people tend to do rituals whenever time and space permits, and for them a different approach works.

Tangible items or tools necessary in a basic ritual are candleholders, incense burners, lighter/matches, self-igniting charcoal, incense, herbs, a bowl of water, and, of course, candles. Intangible items necessary for your ritual are common sense, planning, and intuition.

1. ADVANCE PLANNING

As long as you know your intentions, you can plan your spell or desired outcome. Most importantly, be clear about your intentions. Any state of confusion can jeopardize your outcome. Your mind should be focused and cool for best results. When planning your spell, plan a day and time that is conducive to minimal interruptions, and make sure that you have all your necessary ingredients and tools beforehand. For instance, if you are trying to banish negativity, have the appropriate floor wash, bath materials, incense, and candles ready.

MOON PHASES

If you like to work with the moon, lunar phases are important in determining the best time for magic. The moon's energy is in its strongest influence the day before or the day after either the full moon or the new moon, with the day or night of the actual full or new moon being the most powerful.

For instance, if your calendar states that there will be a new moon on January 3, then January 2 and January 4 will have strong influences, with January 3, the actual day of the full or new moon, having the most powerful influence upon your work. As the moon waxes (when the amount of the illuminated surface of the moon as seen from the earth is increasing), the lunar phases progress from new moon to crescent moon, first-quarter moon, gibbous moon, and full moon. In the northern hemisphere, if the left side of the moon is dark then the light part is growing, and the moon is referred to as waxing (moving towards a full moon). This is a good time to work magic for increase or growth—the ideal time for positive magic. It is also a good time to start projects or to increase psychic energy.

During the waning or dark moon (when the amount of the illuminated surface of the moon as seen from the earth is decreasing), the lunar phases progress from full moon to waning gibbous, last quarter, crescent, and new moon. If the right side of the moon is dark, then the light part is shrinking, and the moon is referred to as waning (moving towards a new moon). The waning moon is a time to cause things to decrease, to remove problems, or to banish negative energies. This is also a good time for study and meditation. By working with the moon's energy instead of against it, you should find yourself in greater harmony and rhythm with the universe on a spiritual level.

2. CANDLES

One of the main ingredients of ritual is candle burning, which provides light and energy to the spirit world. Candles have been used for centuries by almost every culture around the world. They are mystical and magical, and they create a sense of divine intervention from the universal energies that we invoke to help us accomplish our goals. Using candles is a great way to attract the things we need and want or to repel and send away unwanted energies. The ancients, or our elders, have mastered the art of candle burning for a variety of purposes: healing, protection, higher awareness, meditation, etc. Candles are very hypnotic and can help us focus on our intentions, prayers, and desires with greater clarity, which creates an environment for better results. There are many ways in which candles can be used: for meditative purposes; to influence and attract situations in our favor, such as those dealing with love, money, or jobs; or to banish negative or evil influences. However, there is no need to use any type of magic or spiritual work with candles to harm or take away from other people; doing so is asking for harm to reverse back to us in greater amounts.

In candle work, your approach means everything. A candle believe it or not is a creature of nature and a living entity. Its color alone links it to the corresponding elements within nature, as well as the flame, of course, which represents the fire element. Therefore, you should view your candle as your best friend. Talk to your candle and tell it its purpose for it is your great communicator; amplifying and transmitting your desires and wishes into the universe. The act of infusing and lighting your candle is what brings it alive. It is a multidimensional being that operates between the physical and the invisible realms.

One of the main reasons people burn candles is to petition help from their spirit guides. So, don't look at your candle as just a candle. Treat your candle as your spirit helper. As previously stated, your candle becomes a living entity as you work with it and add energy to it. Your ritual work will be much more effective if you view and treat your candle and all your chosen ingredients as the energy beings that they are. As you prepare your candle, cleaning it, charging it, programming it, you are manipulating its energy to help you. You are bringing it to life to be able to interact with the elements within nature and to influence (bring about) your desired outcomes. Your thoughts, energy, prayers, words, oils and herbs add power and character to your candle.

Consistency builds power; so, by burning a candle consistently, you add force and power to your prayers and requests. BUT FIRST *YOU MUST KNOW WHAT YOU WANT!* And, then the next very necessary factor is you must acquire the ability to *FOCUS, FOCUS, FOCUS.* Your capacity to concentrate and hold the image of what you want in your mind's eye (for an extended length of time) is extremely important in manifesting your goals. Your thoughts and objectives *MUST BE CLEAR* so that the universe and your ancestors are *clear* about your intentions and desires. The universe does not care what you intended to do—it will manifest exactly what you project. *For instance, if you want to attract large sums of money then you must be able to see yourself in your mind's eye having large sums of money. Not only do you need to see yourself with the money, but you must feel good about the vision as well. On the flip side, if you can see yourself with large sums of money but then you don't feel worthy inside to have it then your inadequate feelings will override your desire to have loads of cash and this conflict becomes an energetic obstacle making it difficult for the universe and/or spirits to grant your desires. There is no clarity between the vision in your mind's eye and your emotions. The same rule applies if you're seeking a relationship, job, or even protection.*

Again, when making a request, know and be clear about what you are asking to have happen. Sometimes our requests or desires may not be what are ultimately right for us, and the guides may not give us what we want. On other occasions, time may be a factor, and our wishes may come through at later dates. Other times, the spirits may hold out until they think we are ready, and only then will they give us our desired wishes.

Do not forget: Above all, think about safety first, especially if children and animals are around and when working with candles, fire, or heated items.

3. ANOINTING OILS

Condition oils are used to dress or bring power to candles before burning. Oils are also used to repel evil influences or to attract favorable vibrations. You can use anointing oils for the blessing and dressing of objects, such as talismans or amulets. Always consecrate or anoint your candle with a specific purpose in mind. If you want to draw money, use money-drawing oil. You can also add more than one oil to complement or add additional power and focus to your work. Also, there are several ways to anoint a candle, depending on whether you are using an enclosed glass candle or a waxed candle. The most popular anointing method for a waxed or pull-out candle (a candle that can be pulled out of its glass enclosure) is to put a liberal amount of oil in your hands, and, if the candle is for banishing unwanted, crossed, or jinxed conditions, start from the center of the candle and stroke the oil into the candle towards the top. When done, put more oil on your hands and then start from the center again and stroke the oil into the candle towards the bottom. Rub only in one direction, not back and forth. If the candle is for the purpose of attracting something, drawing luck, or drawing positive vibrations, put oil in your hands and, starting from the bottom, stroke the oil into the candle towards the center; then, adding more oil, stroke the candle from the top towards the center. And for the dressing of a glass-enclosed candle, pour some oil on the top of the candle and, if the candle is for banishing, rub the oil into the candle clockwise. If the candle is for attracting or drawing, rub the oil into the candle counter-clockwise.

The most important part of *"charging"* your candle is to concentrate very deeply on the purpose in mind. As with anything, the more effort you put into it, the greater the results.

4. SPIRITUAL CLEANSING BATHS AND HERB BATHS

The importance and purpose of a spiritual cleansing bath or spiritual cleansings in general is to cleanse our *aura* (spiritual body) and personal belongings of negative debris. An *aura* is an invisible field of energy that surrounds the physical body. As a matter of fact, everything in the universe is composed of energy and has an energy field or aura that surrounds it. An aura is different from person to person, from place to place, and from object to object, depending on its vibration, frequency of energy, or character traits.

As humans, we leave traces and imprints of our energy everywhere we go, stand, sit, sleep, touch, and eat. This is why it is extremely important to cleanse items or spaces that once belonged to someone else, such as apartments, cars, clothing, jewelry, offices, etc. You don't want other people's energy to affect you. Spiritual cleansings are prepared to lift, remove, and drive away unwanted negative or malevolent energy by mending and removing all that is not serving your highest interest or divine purpose. The same way you wash bacteria, dirt, debris, oils, and sweat from your physical body, your spiritual body, home, and belongings must be cleansed of dirty energy that can negatively affect you on a daily basis. For instance, you can get a good or bad vibe about a person you have met, a room you have entered, a place you are visiting, or an object that you've touched. Some vibrations will give you the creeps, other vibes will raise your intuitive antenna, and some vibrations will make you feel good, warm, and fuzzy. Aura vibrations will cause you to react either positively or negatively to a particular person, place, or thing depending on the ambience of the energy it emanates.

Your aura is like a fingerprint, completely unique in its expression. Your spiritual body retains information on every soul experience and contains information about your states of being: physical, mental, emotional, and spiritual. Think of your aura as a force field. When you are at your optimum, your force field is strong, making it difficult for negative energies to penetrate and affect your physical being and your outlook on life. But when you feel bad, have no money, are confused, are depressed, are down on your luck, have been ill, are having relationship issues, feel stressed, are going through a crisis, or are experiencing a tragic situation, the aura is substantially weakened, allowing many things, mainly unseen, to attack and damage the spiritual body. Most people are not aware that their aura can be damaged, blocked, distorted, and clogged with negative and inharmonious energies that are picked up in everyday life. After much neglect, your spiritual body becomes "beaten" with breaks, holes, rips, tears, and areas of dark or stagnant energy caused by traumas and emotional, physical, mental, psychic, or spiritual disorders. And although the human body, both physical and spiritual, was designed to heal itself, it is often unable to because of the stresses of modern-day living, environmental toxins, electromagnetic radiations, frustrations, negative social interactions, poor judgments, surrounding conditions, and unhealthy habits that result in the need for major healing and repair work.

We are energy beings; just more dense but spirits can see our energy. They see the colors in our aura and in our body. They sense our vibrations, frequency, and our scent. Like bees to honey - this is what attracts them - this is how they can follow you. And like a dog they can track you. So keeping your aura clean and healthy is important. Keeping your thoughts and feelings positive and on a high note is important. It's hard to live this way 24/7 but living in goodness everyday is a great thing. This means treating people the way you want to be treated; but using your sword when you need to defend yourselves or stepping on the dark side when it becomes necessary to survive. We are also electromagnetic and like a magnet we can attract spirits/entities by our actions. If you are dark in your heart and negative in your mind, then this is what you will attract and vica versa. On the flip side, just because you live in the light and by goodness does not mean that you will _not_ attract anything negative. The "light" attracts all types of pesky bugs like moths, gnats, mosquitoes, etc., and we can attract pesky spirits the same way...

For those who saw the movie, _"Predator"_, remember how the alien was able to track the army men? Remember, how the alien would stop and analyze the body and head of the person before he would strike? The alien saw the men by the colors of the thermal heat emitting from their bodies. If you haven't seen the movie, check it out on YouTube. Well spirits, do the same thing. They look at the colors in our aura. And if it's a bad spirit it can attack you by the weaknesses in your aura and this is why spiritual cleanings are extremely important. This teaches us to be mindful of how we might attract unwanted energies. When bad things happen, check yourself from time to time. Ask yourself, "Is it me, am I thinking or doing something to attract these energies and circumstances? or, "I'm not doing enough to keep these energies from affecting me?" This is a good way to analyze self; checking your state of mind and your thoughts. Our mind, body, spirit, aura, thoughts, feelings, words - attract good and bad.

Spiritual cleansing baths are spiritually infused and hand-prepared with fresh green herbs, plants, perfumes, and powders specifically prepared to bring blessings of opportunity, remove negativity, alleviate a particular problem, and uplift the spiritual and physical body of the person being helped. The following are common remedies that I have used in the beginning stages of my journey, and they have worked for me. Try them; maybe they will work for you as well.

BATH 1 — GUARDIAN ANGEL

BATH A
Ingredients: ½ cup of white flowers, 1 cube of cascarilla, 1 tablespoon of holy water, 1 tablespoon of Florida water (perfume).

Boil white flowers for ½ hour in 6 cups of tap water; let cool. Add cascarilla (eggshell powder), 1 tablespoon of holy water, and 1 tablespoon of Florida water.

BATH B
Ingredients: ½ cup of yerba buena (herb), ½ cup of abre camino (herb), ½ cup of white flowers, 1 tablespoon of holy water, 1 tablespoon of Florida water

Boil herbs and flowers for 1/2 hour in 6 cups of tap water. Let cool. Add Holy water and Florida water.

Bath instructions for all baths: Once mixture is made, if not already in a bowl, pour into a bowl and pray over it your requests and desires. Sit it in bathroom until you are ready for it. Take regular bath first. When done take herbal mixture and pour down over the head, the back, shoulder, arms, torso, legs, etc. While doing this and depending on the bath, you will either be asking for all negativities or evil to be removed or you will be praying for good desires like a job opportunity, love, money spiritual upliftment, clarity of dreams, etc. Do not dry off. Put on light colored clothing, preferably white. Light candle, meditate, prayer and relax preferably for the evening. Light one candle everyday for 7 days. Each time you light candle you will meditate and pray your desires. A significant reason for prayer is to announce and proclaim that all unwanted negative and evil thought forms, energies, or spirits must leave your spiritual space. In your prayers, you can ask God and the spirit protectors to actually help you to rid your self, space, home, or work area of anything unholy. You want to remove anything evil or anything that is not serving your highest interest. You want nothing but vibrations of love, light, goodness, peace, happiness, etc., and to help achieve this, I have included prayers with the baths, floor wash, and incense to provide you with some guidance.

BATH 2 – REFRESHER BATH
TAKE WHENEVER YOU NEED A LIFT

BATH A
Ingredients: ½ of cup of white flowers, ½ of cup of yellow roses, ½ of cup of dried patchouli (herb), 2 cups of tap water
Perfumes: 1 tablespoon of Lavender Water, Lluva de Plata, Spiritual Help, Santa Clara

Boil herbs and flowers for 1/2 hour in 6 cups of tap water. Let cool. Add holy water and all perfumes listed above.

BATH B
Ingredients: ½ cup of white rice, ½ cup of marigolds, and ½ cup of yellow flowers such as mums, carnations, or roses, 1 tablespoon of Kolonia 1800 (perfume)

In a pot, boil rice for 10 minutes with 6 cups of tap water. Pour water off rice and save in a separate bowl. Let cool. If you like, you can add more water to the rice grains and cook them for a meal; this way you will not be wasting the rice. Once the starch water in the bowl has cooled, add the marigolds, yellow flowers, and Kolonia 1800. Mix liquid with your hand, turning clockwise, while saying your prayers and your intentions. It's ready to be used as a spiritual bath.

BATH 3 — CLEANSING/OPEN ROAD BATH

BATH A

Ingredients: ½ of cup of quita maldicion (dried herb), ½ cup of white flowers such as mums, carnations, or roses, cascarilla, 6 cups of tap water.

Boil quita maldicion in 6 cups of tap water for 1 hour, let cool. Add white flowers, breaking up petals with your hands. Crumble the cascarilla into the water, mix, and pray your intentions. Take 1 bath and follow with Bath B the next day.

BATH B

Ingredients: Gather ½ cup of the following herbs: vencedor, abre camino, menta, albahaca, yerba luisa, rompe saraguez
1 tablespoon of Holy water
Perfume: 1 tablespoon of Pompeya

Boil all herbs in 6 cups of tap water for 1 hour and let cool. Add the perfume. Take 1 bath per day for 3 consecutive days.

BATH 4 — OPEN ROAD/PATH BATH

Ingredients: Gather ½ of cup of each herb: abre camino, vencedor, menta, albahaca, yerba buena, artemisa, mejorana
Perfumes: 1 tablespoon of each: Vencedor, Abre Camino, Balsamo Tranquilo, Money, Love

Boil all herbs in 6 cups of tap water for 1 hour and let cool. Add the perfumes. Take 1 bath a day for 3 consecutive days. Remember to pray for your path to be cleared and the obstacles removed.

Bath 5 — Need Cash Bath

Ingredients: Gather ½ of cup of each herb: boton de ore, abre camino, albahaca, yerba buena, artemisa, guanabana
Perfumes: 1 tablespoon of each: Vencedor, Abre Camino, Money, Success, Love

Boil all herbs in 6 cups of tap water for 1 hour and let cool. Add the perfumes. Take 1 bath a day for 3 consecutive days. You can also carry a citrine stone with you afterwards to attract abundance.

Bath 6 — Good Luck Bath

Ingredients: ½ cup of White flowers, ½ cup of lucky leaves, ½ cup of rose petals
Perfumes: 1 tablespoon of each: "One Drop of Luck," Brasis de Caribe, Mr. Money, Fast Luck

Boil flowers, leaves, and petals in 6 cups of tap water for ½ hour and let cool. Add perfumes. Take 1 bath a day for 3 consecutive days.

Bath 7 — Fruit Bath
Take to attract good things, fruitful things

Ingredients: 1 apple, 1 orange, 1 banana, coconut water

Mash apple, orange, and banana. Mix together with coconut water and wash body with mixture. Rinse off with cool water.

Bath 8 — Luck Bath

Ingredients: 5 cinnamon sticks, 5 cloves, ½ cup of different colored flowers (crushed), 1 tablespoon of your favorite perfume, ¼ cup of honey, 1 tablespoon of Florida water, 1 tablespoon of holy water

Boil cinnamon sticks, cloves, and flowers in 6 cups of tap water for ½ hour and let cool. Add perfume, honey, Florida water, and holy water.

BATH 9 — SWEET HERBAL BATH
USE TO ATTRACT THAT SPECIAL SOMEONE

Ingredients: Gather a half handful of each of the following: fresh cardamom seeds, rosemary, fresh orange peel, powdered cinnamon, 4 cups of fresh river water, small bottle of champagne, ½ cup of honey, 1 tablespoon of your favorite perfume or cologne, ½ cup of sweetened condensed milk.

Combine cardamom seeds, rosemary, orange peel, and cinnamon in a mortar. Use the pestle to crush and mix the cardamom, rosemary, orange peel, and cinnamon while praying for the desired attraction to that special someone. Transfer to a bowl and combine with the remaining ingredients; mix with your hands. When done, you can take 1 bath for 3 consecutive days with this.

BATH 10 — HEAVY CLEANSING BATH

Ingredients: Gather ½ cup of the following herbs: apazote, tartago, algodon, rompe murrilla, verbena, quita maldicion, tap water, 1 tablespoon of holy water

Boil all herbs in 6 cups of tap water for 1 hour; let cool. Add holy water. Take 1 bath a day for 7 consecutive days.

BATHS AND CLEANSINGS FOR CHILDREN

Children are like magnets and are very susceptible to absorbing negative energies around them. You could simply wash down child with holy water while praying your intentions to God and the child's guardian angel, or you could fill a bowl with 4 cups of tap water, adding some holy water, cascarilla, and white flower petals that you can break up with your hands. For children over 8 years of age, you can add a little Florida water for fragrance.

5. FLOOR WASHES

Floor washes can be prepared and used in the same manner as spiritual cleansing baths, except floor washes are used to rid your dwelling space of negative influences and to bring positive energy to your living place or workplace. For convenience, you can also use prepared bottled baths and/or floor washes.

FLOOR WASH 1 — REMOVE NEGATIVITY/ PURIFICATION

Ingredients: Bucket of water, ½ cup of sea salt, 1/8 cup of holy water, 1 tablespoon of Florida water

Add sea salt, holy water, and Florida water to a bucket of tap water. Mix clockwise and pray your intentions.

FLOOR WASH 2
REMOVE NEGATIVITY/EVIL INFLUENCES

Ingredients: Bucket of water, 1/8 cup of ammonia, 1/8 cup of holy water, 1 tablespoon of Florida water

Add ammonia, holy water, and Florida water to a bucket of tap water.

FLOOR WASH 3 — REMOVE NEGATIVITY

Ingredients: Bucket of water, crushed camphor, 1/8 of holy water, 1 tablespoon of Florida water

Add crushed camphor, holy water, and Florida water to a bucket of tap water.

FLOOR WASH 4 – EXTREME SITUATIONS WHERE WITCHCRAFT MAY BE INVOLVED

Ingredients: Bucket of water, LaBomba, ammonia, holy water

At your local botanica, ask for a liquid mixture called La Bomba. It smells, but is very strong and powerful. Pour ¼ bottle into a bucket of water. Add a capful of ammonia & holy water.

Mop house from the back to the front door. While mopping through the house, pray that all negativity, confusion, and evil leave and that peace, tranquility, and happiness stay. When you get to the front door, say, *"I dispose and remove all negativity and evil, never to return. In the name of all that is holy, just, and pure in light, love, truth and wisdom."* Or you can conclude in the name of the God or the Deity/Godhead of your culture (Olofi, Allah, Sambi, etc.).

FLOOR WASH FOR FRONT/BACK OF DOOR & STEPS (IF APPLICABLE)

Ingredients: Bucket of cool water, bluing (available as blue balls), sea salt, holy water, Florida water

Add bluing, sea salt, holy water, and Florida water to a bucket of cool tap water. Wash the front side of door and back side of door with mixture. Pray to purify your door from negativity, the evil eye, or anything that may be thrown your way. If you have a house, pour the remaining mixture down the steps or walkway.

6. Incense

The use of incense is an ancient custom and has been utilized in ceremonies for hundreds of years and longer by many cultures and religious institutions. Many practitioners—including spiritualists, mediums, and clairvoyants—believe that incense enhances your ritual, is pleasing to the spirits, and helps to create the right atmosphere. Incense is also used to help you relax and focus upon your desired outcome. Furthermore, it can be burned to dispel bad energy or to attract good energy.

Gums and Resins

Benzoin – Purification
Copal – Purification, Favor, Divination, Induce Trance
Frankincense – Protection, Purification, Spirituality
Myrrh – Protection, Healing, Spirituality
Sage – Absorbs Negativity, Protection, Spirituality
Sandalwood – Protection, Healing, Spirituality
Three Kings Incense – mixture of gums and resins

Dried Herbs or Leaves

Basil – Exorcism, Removal of Evil, Protection
Bay Leaf – Protection, Purification, Strength
Garlic Skins – Exorcism, Purification
Rosemary – Protection, Spirituality
Sage – Purification, Protection
Yerba Buena – Clarity, Peace, Tranquility

7. Miscellaneous Remedies

These include common remedies that can be used to

clear up and absorb negativity or deter bothersome spirits/eguns. When doing these things, remember to pray your intentions or the purpose of using these items. This helps your own guardian spirits know how to help you.

HOLY WATER AND RAIN WATER

For sprinkling around the house. Sprinkle in every corner and every room of the house while praying for peace of home and for all negativity and evil to go away.

FOR CONFUSION OF THE MIND

You can also wash your head in holy water and coconut water. Add cascarilla/efun, mix, pray over it, and wash your head with the mixture so that confusions and negative thought patterns will be minimized.

DOOR ENTRANCES OR BEDTIME

Keep a clear glass of water underneath the bed, next to the nightstand, or by the doorway to absorb potential negativity.

or

Place a glass of water under the bed, on the nightstand, or behind your front door with one of the following added:
- *Alum* – for clarity
- *Bluing* (blue balls) – to remove negativity and bring goodness
- *Camphor* – to remove negativity and clear nightmares

- *Egg* – to absorb any kind of negativity or foul play
- *Florida water* (or any perfume) – to clear negativity and attract goodness

or

Place a glass of water on an upside-down saucer beneath your bed, on your nightstand, or behind your front/back door entrances to reverse negativity or any ill will being sent your way.

EXAMPLES OF CLEANSINGS OUTDOORS

If you cannot light candles where you live, you can buy a lantern candleholder that holds a small tea light.

When you go to the cemetery, park, ocean, etc., you can light the candle there and pray. When finished, put the candle out and take it back home, and the next time you go to that place, light it again. You don't have to choose one of the places I mentioned—it can be anyplace that you feel is sacred. You should make a point to go there on a frequent basis. For instance, if you go to the park or woods at least once a week, light your candle in the lantern, place it on the ground in front of a tree or big rock that you've chosen as your favorite spot, say your prayers for at least fifteen to thirty minutes, make your offerings, and you're done for the week.

Using this small lantern is a very safe way to light a candle for your spirits. If you believe, it will work for you. Use your chosen place as your sanctuary. Let the spirits know that this is the only place you have where you can reach out to them and communicate with them in peace. Also, every night before you go to bed, pray to God, your guardian angel, and spirit protectors for peace and clarity. Pray as much as you can every night. You will see that if you put your heart into it, and if you keep your promises to the spirits, things will start to change for the better.

Cemetery Cleansings

Get nine pieces of various fruit. For example, one apple, one orange, one banana, one pear, one peach, one mango, one plum, one kiwi, and one melon.

Take each piece of fruit, one at a time, hold it in your hands, and pray over it. Pray to God and your guardian angels and spirit protectors to remove any and all evil energies—to let the bad spirits be enticed by the fruit and stay in the cemetery where they belong.

Before entering the cemetery, take nine pennies and throw them in the cemetery, asking the gatekeeper and all of the spirits for blessings for your entrance. Find a good spot in the cemetery or even at the gate of the cemetery if you don't want to go in all the way. One by one, take each piece of fruit and pass it or wipe it all over your body from head to toe—with your clothes on and with the fruit peelings on—and pray that all evil and negativity be removed. Leave all nine pieces of fruit in a pile at the gate of the cemetery or in the cemetery, but not too far in. Take nine pennies and leave them at the pile. It would be good if you could do this near a tree or bush in the cemetery, but at the gate or near the cemetery wall is fine.

On the way out of the cemetery, leave another nine pennies at the gate, thanking the spirits for their help.

Ocean or River Cleansings

You should go to the ocean/beach on a frequent basis if you're able to. Take an entire honeydew melon and rub it all over your body, praying to Yemaya or Olokun, the owners of the sea (if you do not want to call the names of Yemaya or

Olokun, you can just call on the ocean divinities or spirits of the ocean in general), asking them to remove any and all evil from you and to help you. Throw the melon into the ocean and ask Yemaya, Olokun, or the spirits of the ocean to take away all the bad things. When you have finished praying, pour molasses into the ocean and throw in seven pennies.

You can also clean yourself at the ocean with seven pieces of fruit; if you are praying specifically to Olokun, it should be nine pieces of fruit. Take each piece of fruit, one at a time, hold it in your hands, and pray over it. One by one, take a piece of fruit and pass it/wipe it all over your body, from head to toe—with your clothes on and with the fruit peelings on—and pray to God and your guardian angels and spirit protectors that all evil and negativity be washed away by Yemaya and Olokun's waters.

At a river, you will need five pieces of fruit, one of which needs to be an orange, and five pennies. You will follow the instructions above for passing and wiping the fruit all over your body. You will pray to either the spirits of the river in general, or you can pray to the river goddess herself, Oshun, asking her for her many blessings, protection, love, money, etc. When you have finished praying, pour honey in the river and throw in the five pennies. You are done.

VITALIZING FAITH

"In order to have faith, we must have a conviction that all is well. In order to *keep* faith, we must allow nothing to enter our thought which will weaken this conviction. Faith is built up from belief, acceptance and trust. Whenever anything enters our thought which destroys, in any degree, one of these attitudes, to that extent faith is weakened.

Our mind must be steady in its conviction that our life is some part of God, and that the Spirit is incarnated in us. Affirmations and denials are for the purpose of vitalizing faith – for the purpose of converting thought to a *belief* [better yet, a knowing] in things spiritual. The foundation for correct mental treatment is perfect God, perfect man, and perfect being. Thought must be organized to fit this premise, and conclusions must be built on this premise. We must keep our faith vital, if we hope to successfully treat for ourselves or others.

All sciences are built upon *faith principles.* All principles are invisible, and all laws accepted on faith. No man has seen God at anytime, nor has he seen goodness, truth or beauty, but who can doubt their existence?

Not only must we have complete faith in Spirit, and Its ability to know and to do, but we must have complete confidence in our approach to it. We must not be lukewarm in our conviction. *We must know that we know*. We are to demonstrate that spiritual thought force has power over all apparent material resistance, and this cannot be done unless we have abounding confidence in the Principle which we approach.

Pure faith is a spiritual conviction; it is the acquiescence of the mind, the embodiment of an idea, the acceptance of a concept. If we believe that Spirit, incarnated in us, can demonstrate, shall we be disturbed at what *appears* to contradict this? We shall often need to know that the Truth which we announce is superior to the condition we are to change. In other words, *if we are speaking from the standpoint of the Spirit, then there can be no opposition to it*! It is only when we let go of all human will, and recognize the pure essence of the Spiritual Principle incarnated in us, that thought rises above a belief in duality. We should constantly vitalize our faith by the knowledge that the Eternal is incarnated in us; the God Himself goes forth anew into creation through each one of us; and that in such degree as we speak the Truth, the Almighty has spoken!" by Ernest Holmes

CHAPTER 10

PRAYING AND PRAYERS

"The Universe is a Spiritual System. Its laws are those of intelligence. We approach it through the mind, which enables us to know, will and act. Prayer, faith and belief are closely related mental attitudes.

Prayer is a mental approach to Reality. It is not the symbol but the idea symbolized that makes prayer effective. Some prayers are more effective than others. Some only help us to endure, while others transcend conditions, and demonstrate an invisible law which has power over the visible. In so far as our prayer is affirmative, it is creative of the desired results." by Ernest Holmes

How better to begin and end each day than to sincerely pray your intentions to manifest the life you desire or to energize your rituals for added success? The Bible is very clear about the proper way to pray, stating in the Gospel of Matthew, chapter 6, verses 5-8 of the King James version:

When thou prayest, thou shalt not be as the hypocrites are: for they love to pray standing in the synagogues and in the corners of the streets, that they may be seen of men. Verily I say unto you, they have their reward.

But thou, when thou prayest, enter into thy closet, and when thou hast shut thy door, pray to thy Father which is in secret; and thy Father which seeth in secret shall reward thee openly.

Your greatest protection is to pray in secret. Your desires and wants are between you and the Creator; between you and your ancestors/guides. When you tell others of your wants, desires, dreams and goals, you leave yourself open to invisible attack, especially by those closest to you. You place yourself in a position to be energetically/spiritually blocked by those who secretly fear your greatness, for they are envious/jealous, and they will not want you to grow or move forward and upward. They secretly wish for you to fail; misery loves company. So holding your tongue is your greatest asset!

ABOUT PRAYER

"PRAYER IS ITS OWN ANSWER – Cause and effect are but two sides of thought, and Spirit, being ALL, is both cause and effect. Prayer, then, is its own answer. The Bible tells us: "Before they call will I answer." Before our prayer is formed into words, God has already answered, *but if our prayer is one of partial belief [or doubt], then there is only a tendency toward its answer;* if the next day we wholly doubt, then there is no answer at all. In dealing with the Mind, we are dealing with a force that we cannot fool. We cannot cheat Principle out of the slightest shadow of our most subtle concept. The hand writes and passes on, but the writing remains; and the only thing that can erase it is writing of a different character. There is no obstruction one cannot dissipate by the power of Truth.

So we learn to go deeply within ourselves, and speak [pray] as though there were a Presence there that knows; and we should take the time to unearth this hidden cause, to penetrate this inner chamber of consciousness. It is most worthwhile to commune with Spirit—to sense and feel It. The approach to Spirit is direct...through our consciousness.

This Spirit flows through us. Whatever intelligence we have is this Spirit in us. Prayer is its own answer.

We can be certain that there is an Intelligence in the Universe to which we may come, that will guide and inspire us, a love which overshadows. God is real to the one who believes in the Supreme Spirit, real to the soul that senses its unity with the Whole.

Every day and every hour we are meeting the eternal realities of life, and in such degree as we co-operate with these eternal realities in love, in peace, in wisdom, and in joy—believing and receiving—we are automatically blessed. Our prayer is answered before it is uttered." by Ernest Holmes

Many people pray their desires; however, you can also write your requests or desires on a piece of paper that you place under the candle you have chosen to burn at your altar. It is also common in many cultures to write your desires on a piece of a brown paper bag. Whichever you are comfortable with is fine, but before you pray or write your requests, you should invoke the help and guidance of your guardian angel, ancestors, or spirit guides. When working with the ancestors, I suggest that you make a list of the names of all your departed family members (blood relatives). This way you can call their names and petition their help directly. Then mention your ancestors whose names you do not know, including your distant ancestors, asking for their communication, assistance, blessings, and guidance in achieving your desires. When you are done praying and stating your requests, do not forget to thank them for their time, guidance, and assistance.

Another very significant reason for prayer is to announce and proclaim that all unwanted negative and evil thought forms, energies, or spirits must leave your spiritual space. In your prayers, you can ask God and the spirit protectors to actually help you rid your space, home, or work area of anything unholy. You want nothing but vibrations of love, light, goodness, peace, happiness, etc. I have included some sample prayers to provide you with guidance.

ALTAR PRAYER ◎

Descend upon this altar, spirit most high, and bring forth the light of illumination. Let this place be filled with nothing but positive, loving, and free-flowing energy. In the name of all that is holy, just, and pure in light and truth, let this altar/shrine and everything upon it be cleansed and blessed for my intended purpose. Good spirits, as I [sit/stand] in front of my altar/shrine, I call upon the spirit of my guardian angels, ancestors, and spirit guides to be present and to hear my prayers and requests. I bring greetings, and I ask for blessings from all my spiritual guides and teachers in helping me achieve my desires. In the name of the most high, I pray.

[State your request.]

GUARDIAN ANGEL PRAYER

With any kind of spiritual work, you should invoke your guardian angel and spirit protectors at all times, especially when doing work for someone else. It is the job of your guardian angel to protect you; therefore, you should maintain protection at all times to keep safe from attracting negative spirits, entities, or vibrations. Your guardian also opens the way for other guides to assist you.

Guardian angel, God's personal messenger, bring light into my life and guide me down the path that is right for me in this incarnation. Teach me to listen to your voice so that I will always make the right choices for myself and for my loved ones. Take me in your arms, protect me from all harm, and do not let evil cross my path. My sweet, guardian angel, give me the strength and the wisdom to battle the advances of my enemies. Lighten my burdens and help me overcome all the struggles and difficulties in my life. And above all, my guardian angel, hear my prayers and illuminate me with your divine light and blessings, always.

[Say your request.]

Good Spirits Prayer

I call upon my guardian angel and the good spirits who surround me, particularly my superior guide, to intercede before God on my behalf. I am a human person of many errors, but I open myself to your guidance and correction. I seek your communication; therefore, I come to you with humility and devotion, leaving my thoughts and actions of the world's way to the side. I call upon you with utmost love and respect from my heart, and I would ask for you to please come, good spirits, and commune with me for the betterment of myself and all others. I ask this with faith and sincerity in the name of the most high, I pray.

Ancestor Prayer – General

Libations (with water, liquor, or wine) are poured, incense is burned, prayers are made, and honor is given—all in hopes of awakening and earning favors from our dead ancestors to garner blessings and hinder misfortunes.

> *Ancestors, I pour libations, I pray and offer light to you—especially to those spirits that need it most—and I ask Olodumare, God, to fortify your spirit and that the light of divine protection always be around you. Ancestors, let God's infinite power elevate every essence of your being so that you can intercede and help us here on earth, and may God have mercy on us all to grant the ancestors and the guardian spirits permission to help fulfill my prayers and my requests. In the name of the most high, I pray.*

◎ ANCESTOR PRAYER I

As I sit/stand in front of my altar, I call upon the spirits of my ancestors. I call upon my ancestors from near and from far. I call upon my distant ancestors and those recently deceased. I call upon all those I know and remember and all those I have forgotten but whose blood runs through my veins. Greetings and good blessings to:

[Say the names of your ancestors.]

I've come to ask for your continued blessings and for you to hear my prayers. Ancestors, I ask that you walk before me so I can avoid straying and being lost. Walk before me as my guide around the pitfalls and traps of my enemies. Walk before me as a beacon light so that I may never know darkness. Walk before me so that I may follow your example of pride and humility. Walk before me with patience, for I may not always be able to keep up.

Ancestors, I welcome your communications, and I ask that you help my family and me with all our daily difficulties. I ask that you help me remove my obstacles with minimal pain and suffering. I welcome your guidance and instruction with all sincerity, and I promise my best to learn your teachings and heed your warnings. Ancestors, there's no love like family love, and I ask that you continue loving and protecting me, keeping me safe and peaceful always.

With blessings from our divine parent, I will pray for your continued elevation always. In the name of the most high, I pray.

ANCESTOR PRAYER II

Mighty ancestors, you are the symbol of my lineage; therefore, I call upon you to step in and guide my life. I ask that you walk by my side so that I come to know that I am never alone. You are deceased, but God's power makes you mighty in your own way. Grab hold of the divine light so that you can protect my family and me from the dangers and sufferings of the world. Protect us from evil and cleanse us of the troubles we bear.

Ancestors known and unknown, help me understand the essence of prayer and spirit so that I can understand you as a way to understand myself. Give me insight and vision in the face of insurmountable odds so that I can obtain the things I need to live comfortably, and teach me from your invisible world so that I can manifest fruitfully in all areas of my life. Help me understand your great wisdom so that our lessons will remain forever alive. In the name of the most high, I pray.

ANCESTRAL HEALING PRAYER

You may feel uncomfortable or bitter about venerating ancestors who have been abusive in some way or another, whether emotionally, physically, sexually, or verbally. It is understandable why you would not want to venerate an ancestor who has caused you or a loved one harm, but I ask that you attempt to forgive the person any way you can. Although this is easier said than done, know that the act of forgiveness will bring the energy of the *wrongful act into the light*, freeing you to heal. In addition, many ancestors who have done wrong in life will seek light and prayer from you, wanting forgiveness and repentance, and will want to give, help, and do what they did not get to do in life, all because they have come to realize their mistakes while residing on the other side. However, and in any case, the healing is needed for both the deceased and the living so that the abusive patterns will cease, no longer plaguing members of the family line, directly or indirectly.

In many cases, when negative energies are not healed, this karmic energy will affect both the individual and the whole generational line. You can probably think of one family that just cannot get it together—they struggle and suffer for many reasons. Some families carry a karmic energy of financial problems, while in other families, drugs and judicial problems are prevalent. Whether through prayers, rituals, or ceremonies, we can work to heal our ancestors in the spirit realm so that they can help us heal in the living realm. For this reason, I have written an ancestral healing prayer to help both the living and the deceased heal.

✦ The Ancestral Healing Prayer says:

I offer light and pour libation with respect and honor for all my ancestors whose names I know, [say all the names that you know], and whose names I don't know, to uplift and liberate their souls in the name and light of the Almighty God. For it is through the love, will, and power of God that all souls are saved.

I offer prayer and protection by way of the divine Creator for those ancestral souls and spirits that are in darkness, forgotten, or lost. Let the light I offer fade out the shadows of fear and guide you toward the arms of God.

I offer guidance to my ancestors and spirits by way of the guardian angels and protective spirits who, by the power and order of God, will assist them in their greater act of evolution. Let the light I offer be a beacon of hope and serve as an escape and protective shield from the shadows of despair.

I offer love, compassion, and comfort to those ancestral souls and spirits that are suffering and depressed. Let the light I offer lead them from discord and the miseries of their souls to the sanctuary of God and the joys of heavenly bliss.

I offer healing by way of the supreme being on all spiritual levels for those ancestors and spirits who were abused, afflicted, deceived, enslaved, hated, lonely, misguided, neglected, oppressed, pained, saddened, traumatized, and died tragically or by suicide. Let the light I offer to their souls inspire clemency, liberation, faith, love, and harmony from today onward.

I offer forgiveness to the ancestral souls and spirits that want to sincerely repent for the errors of their ways in the realms of life and death. Let this light guide them to the truth, enlightenment, and righteousness of God.

In addition, I forgive those ancestors who committed wrongs that have set their generational line—those that are living—in barrenness. And I forgive those ancestors whose past sins I've had to suffer as a result of their own naivety, ignorance, and inferior habits and traits. Let the light I offer serve as a reminder for those of us in the living to acknowledge and learn to not make the same mistakes as the ones who lived before us.

In every way, I forgive those ancestors and spirits who need it most so that their souls will embrace, in positive gratification, a new and improved way of living in the spirit realm, and that those souls will elevate in peace and awaken to eternal life as God promised.

In the name of God and through his mercy and blessings, let today be the beginning of a continual healing process for all my ancestral guides and the release of all blocked and negative genetic energy patterns within the generational line, steadily healing each family member, including myself, day by day. As you, the ancestors, heal on the other side, we ask that you forgive us as you have been forgiven and help us to heal with free-flowing, positive, and progressive energy for the better well-being of all concerned.

In the name of all that is holy, just, and pure in light, truth, wisdom, and knowledge, I pray. May the power and peace of God be with us always; in the name of the most high, I give praise.

FOR THE EXPIRED

God of the most high, we call upon you at this present moment, and we ask for your benevolence and grace. We ask that you hear our prayers. Hear, oh lord, that we call upon you and the holy angels for blessings and the power to help the spirit of [name of person] cross over into the light, into your loving arms, and ascend to his/her proper realm.

Divine parent, send your holy angels through the realms to find the soul of [name of person]. This soul may be lost, confused, and scared. God of light and love, have mercy upon this soul that is destitute of spiritual aid and which desires goodness. Help him/her find his/her way into the security of your light, love, and grace. Give eternal rest and peace unto [name of person] and let your perpetual light shine upon him/her. All this we ask in the name of the all that is holy, just, and pure in light, love, truth, and wisdom. In the name of the most high, I pray.

PSALM OF DAVID 61: 1-4

Hear my cry, O God; listen to my prayer. From the ends of the earth I call to you, I call, as my heart grows faint; lead me to the rock that is higher than I. For you have been my refuge, a strong tower against the foe. I long to dwell in your tent forever *and take refuge in the shelter of your wings.*

PRAYER OF LIGHT

Divine parent, most holy above all, I am your humble child and I seek forgiveness for all my wrongdoings, intentional or unintentional. I ask forgiveness for any unclean thoughts or actions that I may have directed towards any of my fellow man.

Divine parent, let your light, the holy light, rain down on me to cast away the shadows of darkness and despair that could be preventing me from elevating in mind, body, and soul. May the power of divine light and love illuminate my entire being so that the energy of evil and negativity will not have any influence on my mind or body. Let the light of God touch me and cleanse me on a cellular level to cast away all negativities and fears that may block me from progress and prosperity in all areas of my life.

Let the light of the holy angels cast away the darts of the evil eye that have been placed upon me and my possessions as targets of jealousy and envy from those who can have the same as I, if only they believed the power of God as the Creator and giver of all things. And God! Let the intensity of your divine light fill the darkest recesses of my mind, my body, and my life so that I can openly love and adore you in my own special way.

And lastly, holy God, shine forth and give me the courage to open my life to new ways of seeking out your loving guidance and to love others more deeply and passionately. In the name of all that is holy, just, and pure in light, I pray.

CLEANSING PRAYER

I call upon the power of the most high and the power of my spirit protectors to bless this bath/floor wash that I have prepared to purify me/my children/my home. In God's holy name, let this mixture be blessed and purified for my intended purpose. I call upon my guardian angel to give me the strength and the energy to charge these ingredients with love, positivity, and nothing but goodness so that all negativity and evil influences will be turned away and removed from my body/ my child's body/my home.

Divine parent, please empower and illuminate my guardian spirits. May the light of God always shine upon them? And good spirits, charged by God to protect me, as I wash my body/my child/ my home with this spiritual mixture, drive away from me/my child/ my home any and all unclean influences and wicked spirits, whoever or whatever they may be. In the name of all that is holy, just, and pure in light, replace this evil and negative energy with nothing but good, healthy, loving, and progressive energy. In the name of the most high, I pray.

EMPLOYMENT PRAYER I

Guardian angel, I call upon you in my time of need. I ask you to hear me and come unto me. I pray for the job that is best suited for me to come, immediately, at this time. I need your divine help and guidance to help me gain suitable employment. Please put the right devices, such as newspapers, e-mail, telephone, and other tools, and the right people in my path. Good spirits, please supply me with a remedy at this time so that I can continue to provide for myself and my family—to keep daily bread on my table. I ask this or something better in the name of all that is holy, just, and pure in light, love, and wisdom. In the name of the most high, I pray.

EMPLOYMENT PRAYER II
BY SONYA I. PERKINS

As I embark on new areas in my life, I ask for the blessings and guidance of God, my ancestors, my spirit guides, and guardian angels. I ask for their blessings to guide me through this difficult period in my life. May I walk through this time with my head held high and with faith in myself and in spirit, and may I survive hard times as my ancestors survived hard times.

I ask in the name of God for assistance in my search for suitable and gainful employment. I ask that my ancestors hear my pleas and put the right devices into my path, such as advertisements and people like recruiters, and that word of mouth reach my ears if the work is right for me.

I ask that whatever opportunities are looking to find someone, let that opportunity find me, for I will be grateful for the blessing that opportunity will bequeath me. I ask that opportunity search and find me, as I have searched and searched for employment. They say opportunity knocks, but only one time. My eyes are open to see opportunity; my ears await the sound of opportunity knocking. I am ready to receive opportunity. I have patience, and I will continue to search for the job/career that is right for only me.

I seek employment not just for a paycheck but also to be a productive, contributing member of my community. I ask for a suitable job, so that I may take care of my loved ones and myself. I ask for work to come to my hands so that I may feel and be useful. I ask that the people I work with be decent, friendly, hard working, and easy to get along with. I ask that I be compensated accordingly for the work that I provide. I ask that the job I secure will be something that I can look forward to doing on a daily basis.

In the name of the divine providence, may my roads be opened and clear for me to find the right job. In the name of my spirit guides, I pray that the door of opportunity be opened to me as I try to become a more productive being. In the name of my guardian angel, I ask that you assist me during the hard times and help me to make it through until suitable employment is held securely in my hands.

In the name of the most high and all that is light, I ask for these blessings for myself and for all those in search of employment for the betterment of all. So it was spoken, so it shall be. Àṣe o!

EMPOWERMENT PRAYER

I break and release all karmic and spiritual ties to any individual or situation that is hurtful, destructive, and non-beneficial in my life.

I break and release all negative thought patterns on all levels of consciousness that are hurtful, destructive, and non-beneficial to my way of life.

I break and release all connections, ties, and links on all levels of existence that block or hinder my progress and receptivity of all good things.

I repel negativity. God is my power supply, and the universe is my enforcer; therefore, I am empowered to attract nothing but great things in my life. In the name of the most high, I pray.

FEMININE POWER
SPIRIT LADIES PRAYER
(INSPIRATIONS FROM THE GODDESSES OF THE WORLD) DEDICATED TO MY GODSISTER, S. PERKINS

Lady spirits of mine, you are special and loved above all the others. So beautiful, and yet, so serene. Charitable spirits, that's who you are, and with your undying love for me, have mercy on my soul and help me with all the difficulties that are in my path. Give me the fervor to come to you always, even in my worst condition.

Lady spirits of mine, you represent all women—the ultimate female energy, goddesses of the world, protective and nurturing in every way. Protect me and keep all danger and harm from me. Keep envy and jealousy away from me. Keep all evil and witchcraft away from me.

Let not my enemies have any power over or against me. It is you who will care for me, for I am forever your child.

Lady spirits of mine pay special attention to me, for I do not always know my way. When I hold my head down, lift it up for me. When I am lost, confused, and swayed off track, with your gentleness guide me back to the path that is right.

Sweet and creative spirits, with your watery and cool influences, cover me and give me the clarity of vision, the confidence, and the strength to walk through this life on an everyday basis. Let me be prosperous — mentally, emotionally, financially — in love and in health. Let your creativity and moral fiber engulf me so that I can exemplify your very existence. And with your power, reveal to me what is known and unknown so that I can plan, and protect my family and me from the visible and invisible forces of the universe that affect my life for good and bad.

And in return, for always being so good to me, I ask in the name of the most high, the Creator of all, to always bless you and cover you with omnipotent light, with all sincerity from my heart in peace and blessings always.

FORGIVENESS PRAYER

Jesus said to God the father, "Forgive them, for they know not what they do." God, you have us here and the weight of the world is upon our shoulders. And sometimes, we as humans are forgetful and neglectful and make mistakes that may offend you, our spirit guides, ourselves, and others, intentionally or unintentionally. Therefore, I ask the divine parent, my guardian angel, and spirit guides to forgive me for my faults and my shortcomings, for I am only human, and sometimes I know not what I do.

Forgive me for my misguided intentions; forgive me for not living up to or keeping promises I may have made; and forgive me, divine parent and good spirits, for not thanking you enough for your guidance as the unseen hand that directs my life in total love and goodness.

Divine parent, I ask forgiveness for all my wrongdoings, past and present. Please bless my better character aspects so that I will grow and have the wisdom and the knowledge to help others. I ask God and the good spirits to open the roads of opportunity to me because I have made a conscious effort to improve my being. And I recognize, my guardian angel, that God appointed you my overseer for many known and unknown reasons, but I specifically need you to help me to eliminate the errors of my ways, as long as I am open and accepting of your teachings and guidance, trying my best to stay on the right path. In the name of the most high, I pray.

HEALTH & HEALING PRAYER

Divine parent, we call upon you and our superior guides in the name of all that is holy, just, and pure in light, love, truth, and wisdom. We ask that you manifest your great healing force in our lives and continue to protect us from all the dangers, sickness, and infirmities of the world. Keep us, dear God, in perfect health in mind, body, and spirit.

Today, Lord, we seek your help on behalf of [full name] who is ill from [name of illness]. We call forth the healing angels to stand at the side of [first name], who needs strength and comfort in this time. Merciful God, source of all health, accept our prayers and light from this candle as energy to grant [first name] the help of your healing power so that his/her sickness may be cured and turned to perfect health. We also ask that you transform our sorrows into joy through our faith in you as the divine physician and healer of the sick.

Angels of healing guide the doctors and nurses with steady hands and ensure they give [first name] the proper diagnosis and prescriptions for a speedy recovery. May [first name]'s heart be filled with confidence that, though he/she may be afraid, you are there with the guardian angels to stand watch and lead charge over the stability and health of his/her mind, body, and spirit. We ask the holy angels to surround and fill [first name]'s body with divine light so that every cell and organ is restored to optimum health. We thank God and the holy angels for their divine help and mercy. And God, grant us the grace to acknowledge your holy will and know that whatsoever you do, you do for the love of us. We ask all this in the name of the most high. Amen

INSPIRATIONAL PRAYER - I AM INSPIRATION

Divine Parent, help me to love myself when I do not feel it from anyone else. God of truth and wisdom, help me to be true to myself when I have doubts or when I am in denial, and give me the strength to see and acknowledge what is real.

God of compassion, help me to believe in myself when others are not sure. Help me to see the beauty in myself when I am feeling my worst; and help me to appreciate the gift that I am to the world when the world cannot see.

God of light and love, give me the power to remove the burdens in my life, for I give them to you. Life is the most precious gift; therefore, give me the strength to hold it dear with utmost value for all others and myself. And divine parent, reveal to me your very existence so that I can build and rebuild my faith in you and in myself, because I know, God, that you love me, and in your eyes, I am truly great.

Through your power – I am a powerful being
Through your grace – I will walk gracefully among others
Through your humility – I, too, will be humble

Through your forgiveness – I will also forgive
Through your love – I, too, can give and receive love in kind
Through your beauty – I personify beauty from within
Divine parent, Creator of all, let my mind, my heart, and my soul be aligned with the greatest power of all—YOU! And through your greatness, I will stand tall in the world as a gift and proof of your abundant love. Because of you as most divine, I AM INSPIRATION!

I RISE ABOVE

I sit in front of my ancestral shrine and I close my eyes. I see myself rising above all that tries to hold me down. I rise above all my obstacles and my fears. I rise above the evil eyes and negative spirits and energies forced upon me. I rise above my oppressors. I rise above all those who only want to suck the life out of me and leave me for dead. And while I am above, I look down and with my heart I connect to the Earth Mother in sincerity and honesty. I ask for her mercy and her grace. I ask the Earth Mother to support me in all that I need and want. I ask her to help to manifest great things in my life – to protect my every step and to keep me safe from all harm. May it be so in the name of all that is holy and just.

LOVE PRAYER

Spirit of loneliness, hear me; spirit of desperation, hear me; spirit of grief, hear me; spirit of depression, hear me; spirit of the unloved, hear me, for I know that I am worthy and deserving of love and affection.

Divine parent, you are the Creator of all, and I know that you created a significant other out there to love me—to care for me.

Sometimes, divine parent, we blind ourselves to giving or receiving love out of pain or out of fear, and if I am closed and sheltered, I ask that you help me open myself to a loving and caring person. But first, dear God, help me love and care for myself so that I can recognize real love when I see it.

God most high, everyone wants to be loved and everyone wants companionship, but sometimes, out of carelessness and desperation, we choose the wrong mate. Sometimes we choose what we think we want and not necessarily what we need. Superior guides, please help me sort through the confusion and guide me in making the right choice.

With my eyes, let me see what is right. Let me be able to see through all the nonsense of those who feed off vulnerable hearts.

With my ears, let me hear all the sweet nothings that I deserve to hear, and let no person hinder my self-confidence or disrespect me with bad or negative words.

With my heart, let me know when I have the right person in my path. And shield my heart from all unnecessary pain distributed by any thoughtless being.

And, divine parent, until that time comes, continue to give me your unconditional love and grace. I know that I am not alone with you and my guardian angel by my side. I ask in the name of all that is holy, just, and pure in light and love. In the name of the most high, I pray.

LOVE BLESSING PRAYER

In the name of all that is holy, just, and pure in light, love, truth, and wisdom, I invite my guardian angel and superior guides to come and help me. I pray to the spirit most high that my physical and spiritual life be repaired and strengthened to bring forth my desires of LOVE. Let all negative emotions, thoughts, and spiritual blocks be removed so that my mind, body, and heart will be open to heal, feel, and receive the order of true love.

I pray, divine parent, that the light of god surrounds me and protects me from any and all dark forces that want to steer me from my goal of love. Negativity has no place in my life and I pray that I can open my heart and soul to the in-flow of love from all that is good and kind. Teach me, divine parent, the meaning of love within and help me to understand my need for a good, loving, and supportive relationship.

I release all negative thoughts, feelings, and fears that I have about love on all the levels of my soul, and no matter whose fault, I forgive and let go of all hurt, pain, and guilt of the past so that the gift of love will find me, shower me, and bring comfort to my life. I ask God most high to show me the way, clear my path, and open the way for me to find my soul mate, and for my soul mate to find me, for my eyes are open to recognize and find that special someone who will be a pleasure and asset in my life. With gratitude, I pray in the name of the most high, I pray.

MONEY BLESSING PRAYER

In the name of all that is holy, just, and pure in light, love, truth, and wisdom, I invite my guardian angel and superior guides as messengers of God to come and help me. I pray to God that my life and my financial outlook be repaired and strengthened to bring forth my desires of increased finances.

Lord, I humbly surrender my financial affairs and concerns about money to your divine care and love. As I increase my knowledge of money management, help me lessen my worries, anxieties, and fears about money and replace them with faith and trust that my debts will be paid and unlimited amounts of money will flow into my life.

I am grateful and I now release and cut all my karmic

ties and negative thought-forms about money, for I know that prosperity is my true state. I am grateful for all the money I have now and the overflow of cash that is coming my way. Bless me, divine parent, with financial prosperity so that I can care for myself and my loved ones and all those who enter into my path who can also benefit from my blessings. In the name of the most high, I pray. Amen.

OPEN DOOR PRAYER

Guardian angel and protecting spirits please open all doors, roads, pathways, and portals to opportunity on all levels of human existence for my family, my loved ones, and myself.

Superior and good spirits, through your energy and power, I will prosper in blessings, health, finances, love, good luck, and worth. Please shield all my possessions, spiritual and material, from evil eyes, negative thought forms, or the witchcraft of my enemies.

And protective spirits please close and keep closed all doors, roads, pathways, and portals to any event, person, force, or entity of any sort that would stand in the way of completing my destiny in this incarnation. In the name of the most high, I pray.

PROSPERITY PRAYER

Divine parent, I am trying to examine the areas of my life that are not successful. Everywhere I turn, I feel blocked. God, I am trying to have faith, but I feel that my means and my resources are at the bare minimum, and I cannot seem to get out of this struggle, nor do I have the strength to remove or move around my obstacles.

Divine parent, if I am not prosperous because of my own doing, please let my guardian angel help me see and take the *right course of action. Good spirits please help me get disciplined in the necessary areas of my life so that I can build the foundation needed to bring me prosperity on all levels. I know that I am fully responsible for my actions, and I know that I need the determination and faith to resolve my issues, but I am asking that you guide and help me keep my mind focused on completing my goals.*

Superior angels, if there is anything (spirit or otherwise) or anyone blocking my prosperity, then I ask that you show me so that I can properly fix the situation. If there are any negative, manipulated, or karmic influences not intended or destined for me, then I ask you, my guardian angel and spirit protectors, by the power of God, to please help and work to remove this bad energy that has entered my path in error, and to bring or redirect the energy that is correct and that God intended only for me.

May God and the good spirits bless me with health, mental prosperity, emotional prosperity, and financial prosperity so that I can take care of myself, my home, my loved ones, and all those who enter into my path and who can also benefit from my blessings. In the name of the most high, I pray.

PRAYER FOR PROTECTION
BY MIGNON GRAYSON-FAGAINS

Oh great spirit, Creator of all that is, please be with us now and forever. In the name of God, the Creator, we invoke the most high divine forces of protection.

We call upon the powers and the archangels of protection from the highest divine rank. Powers, spirits, and archangels of protection, missionaries of the most high, we call upon you to create a shield—a blanket of protection around [insert names, place, or event]. Cover us and wrap us in your love and mercy. We are in need of this protection today and all days.

There are energies, forces, spirits, people, thoughts, and wishes that are negative and want to do harm and wish us to fail in our positive progress and endeavors on this earth plane. They are waiting for the first opportunity — the first moment of weakness — to attack. Please remove from us the fears, doubts, and dark thoughts that attract them to us so they may pass us by. Bathe us in light.

We ask for the most high spiritual divine power to protect, fortify, and strengthen us against these and all negative influences now and always. We thank you, Creator, for the protective forces and for their divine work in the name of all that is sacred and holy. Please stand by us in our time of need, now and forever. In the name of the most high, we pray.

PRAYER TO BREAK CURSES

A curse is an evil or a set of bad circumstances that comes upon someone. According to the Bible, if a person is under a curse, evil has come upon them in some way. Many believers of this theory feel that certain problems in life, such as illness, poverty, misfortunes, tragedy, and death, are due to curses targeted to affect an individual or an entire family for generations to come.

This does not mean that every difficult circumstance we encounter is from a curse. God and our guides daily lead us through difficult circumstances as tests for our own good, to help us become stronger in faith and character. We even curse or jinx ourselves at times, being our own worst enemies because of the negativity in our minds and because of the negative words that we speak. But I am referring to an evil curse that comes not from the hand of God but from the enemy. Curses are usually sent from people filled with malice, misery, evil, and hatred. A curse can be ignited through spoken words or through more planned and intended works of witchcraft, projected at a specific person or group of persons to cause harm.

If you feel that either you or someone you know has been cursed, this prayer may help alleviate some of the pressures of this negative and unclean energy.

All powerful God, Creator of all, you have authorized and armed me to do your will and I call upon you in my time of need. By the power, light, and love of God, I ask the Creator to forgive me of any wrongdoings that I have committed against myself, my family, or my fellow brothers and sisters, knowingly or unknowingly. I ask God to look upon me and give me the strength to open my mind, my heart, and my soul toward repentance, and lord, I have confidence that you will forgive me. I recognize, God, that I am not worthy of your favors, but you are a God of compassion and forgiveness, and I come to you with all confidence and sincerity that you will not turn your back on me, for my heart is sincere.

Divine parent, I ask that you lend me your holy shield and your sword of faith so that I will have the strength and protection I need to combat Satan and his henchmen. I call upon the holy angels, the righteous angels, the angels of light, the angels of love, and the angels of judgment and justice to seek out, expose, and destroy all schemes and devices of a spiritual nature that have been sent and used against my family or me. Satan and all spirits of bad nature, I deem you powerless in my life, for I am a child of the living God, and I proclaim your works in my life (and in the lives of my family, my friends, and others) to be absolutely and utterly destroyed.

And in the name of all that is holy, just, and pure in light, I break all individual and generational curses, works of witchcraft, or negative thought forms on all levels of consciousness sent against me, my family, my friends, and others. I ask that God's holy angels and my spirit protectors use God's infinite power to continue to break all works of evil, witchcraft, black magic, mental and spiritual manipulations, or thought forms sent to distract, harm, bind, or destroy me/us. With the help of my warrior angels, I will resist all evil powers sent to me/us from any man, woman, child, spirit, or entity that exists within the universe.

I humbly pray, by the power of God, that all evil of any nature be destroyed in God's name, for my/our soul will not be ruined. I pray for and I bless anyone who is cursing me/us, and I claim them for salvation and eternal life through the power and light of all that is superior in divine love, wisdom, and elevation. In the name of the most high, I pray.

PRAYER TO RELEASE FROM BONDAGE

If you feel that you or someone you know has been tied by the enemy, then the following prayer may be of some help to you.

God, all powerful and all knowing, hear my prayers; hear my cry when I call. Divine parent, [name of person] has been placed in bondage for selfish and malicious gain, and we ask by the power of all that is holy and just that he/she be released.

Superior spirits and protecting spirits, we ask that you break the chains that hold [name of person], the chains that an evil, selfish, and thoughtless person/persons has/have placed on him/her. Let not the words of domination have any affect on [name of person]. We need the power of the holy spirit and the holy angels to remove any and all spiritual manipulations placed upon [name of person] so he/she can do his/her own will and the will of God.

And finally, we ask, divine parent, that his/her guardian angel and spirit protectors gain the light, strength, and power necessary to fight the bad and evil spirits that were commanded to hinder [name of person]'s body, mind, heart, and soul. Let God's holy angels render these bad and evil spirits powerless to harm, bind, distract, or destroy [name of person]'s life. In the name of the all that is holy, just, and pure in light, let [name of person] be freed. In the name of the most high, I pray.

PRAYER TO RELEASE NEGATIVITY IN LOVE/FRIENDSHIPS

On all levels of consciousness, I break all ties and connections with [name of person] and any negative relationships of my past. I break all negative patterns of how I choose men/women/relationships in general.

I release any and all residual feelings I have for [name of person] I ask forgiveness for myself, and I forgive [name of person], as well, for any misunderstandings or hard feelings that may be lingering. May the power of divine light and love illuminate my entire being so that the energy of evil and negativity will not have any influence on my mind or body, obstructing my emotional, mental, or physical advancement.

I wish no harm to come to anyone, and I am open to loving myself and accepting new and positive men/women/relationships in general into my life. May I progress in love and in life for a better way of living—peaceful in heart and content within myself. In the name of the most high, I pray.

PSALM OF DAVID 59 - DELIVERANCE FROM ENEMIES
(MY PERSONAL FAVORITE AGAINST THE HAND OF THE ENEMY)

1. Deliver me from mine enemies, oh my God: defend me from them that rise up against me. 2. Deliver me from the workers of iniquity, and save me from bloody men. 3. For, lo, they lie in wait for my soul: the mighty are gathered against me; not for my transgression, nor for my sin, O LORD. 4. They run and prepare themselves without my fault: awake to help me, and behold. 5. Thou therefore, O LORD God of hosts, the God of Israel, awake to visit all the heathen: be not merciful to

any wicked transgressors. 6. They return at evening: they make a noise like a dog, and go round about the city. 7. Behold, they belch out with their mouth: swords are in their lips: for who, say they, doth hear? 8. But thou, O LORD, shalt laugh at them; thou shalt have all the heathen in derision. 9. Because of his strength will I wait upon thee: for God is my defense. 10. The God of my mercy shall prevent me: God shall let me see my desire upon mine enemies. 11. Slay them not, lest my people forget: scatter them by thy power; and bring them down, oh lord our shield. 12. For the sin of their mouth and the words of their lips let them even be taken in their pride: and for cursing and lying, which they speak. 13. Consume them in wrath, consume them, that they may not be: and let them know that God ruleth in Jacob unto the ends of the earth. 14. And at evening let them return; and let them make a noise like a dog, and go round about the city. 15. Let them wander up and down for meat, and grudge if they be not satisfied. 16. But I will sing of thy power; yea, I will sing aloud of thy mercy in the morning: for thou hast been my defense and refuge in the day of my trouble. 17. Unto thee, oh my strength, will I sing: for God is my defense, and the God of my mercy.

PRAYER TO OPEN A SPIRITUAL GATHERING

Before you start your gathering, set a temporary altar as a focal or meeting point for the living and those in the spirit realm. Place one large glass/goblet of water in the middle and then place one stick candle on the left side of the water and one stick candle on the right side of the water. A bouquet of white flowers would make a nice touch.

When you place the glass or goblet of water, say:
As I place this water, let it represent the love and coolness of our mind, body, and spirit.
When you light the candle on the right, say:
I light this candle to represent the goodness and purity of

those in the spirit realm.

When you light the candle on the left, say:

I light this candle to represent the goodness and purity of our intentions from all those present.

God, almighty and all-knowing, we pay homage to you as the creator of all things rational or irrational, animate or inanimate, material or immaterial. Divine parent, we adore you as the giver of life and the final judge in death. At this time, God of light, we wish to solicit communications from our holy ancestors, our guardian angels, and the superior spirits that surround us. Let it be the will of God and the sincerity of our hearts that our ancestors and guardian angels respond to our call. As we implore the good spirits to come to our aid, we open ourselves to their communication on all levels of consciousness, and we ask the angels to supply us with messages of divine knowledge and wisdom.

In unyielding faith, we gather in the name of God with pure intentions using our faculties of mediumship to intercede between the living and the dead. A gift given to us by our divine parent, who has also commanded the good spirits to be amongst us and to guide us in our efforts of becoming better in who we are. During our spiritual development, may we acquire the strength to remain humble and unselfish in the use of the spiritual powers and gifts that God has afforded us.

And as we have lit our candles, let the flame represent the light of God so that the bad spirits will have no interference in this session, except to seek clemency from their malevolent ways. Let the spirits on a higher order help those weaker and inferior to be inspired by the light, love, and goodness that surrounds them. We pray with fervor and confidence so that the good spirits will guide and protect us from any and all inferior spirit influence or suggestions of evil.

Let all who have gathered here be positive in mind and thought, with full concentration on the deed at hand and with the ability to see beyond the five senses with clean and clear thoughts. We ask our ancestors, our guardian angels, and superior spirits for their insight for our highest good. We ask our guides to teach us and show us what we need to learn. And, as we work by the example of the superior spirits, let none of us be found in error, but if by circumstance we are, then let one amongst us be inspired to help and give correction to that error.

We ask that our ancestors, guardian angels, and spirit protectors bring us in perfect alignment with God. We ask this in the name of all that is holy, just, and pure in light and love. In the name of the most high, I pray.

PRAYER TO CLOSE - A SPIRITUAL GATHERING

We thank all the ancestors, spirit guides, and teachers who came to give guidance and instruction. We implore the good spirits to help us put into practice the teachings that were given and to feel the strength necessary to empower our lives going forward.

We thank you, good spirits, for your visit and your messages. We thank you for your love and your lessons. Lastly, we thank you for your protectiveness.

Also, we ask the superior guides and good spirits to encourage the inferior spirits, who may have attended this meeting, to elevate themselves toward the goodness, light, and love of God.

We now ask you, the spirits, to go with light, That you go with love,

And that you go with peace and coolness.

As we leave this gathering, we ask that our guardians protect us and watch over us for a safe journey home, and that they keep us safe and in good health until we meet again. We ask this in the name of the most high in peace and blessings always.

PRAYERS FOR CHILDREN

All human bodies should be honored, no matter at what age death has occurred, but this section is specific to the departed children, especially the unborn children, whether miscarried or aborted. I feel it is very necessary to touch on this subject because many parents, especially mothers, do not think to pray for or honor the spirits of their unborn children. In the parents' minds, the children were never physically born into the world. Many parents are not aware that even the spirit of an unborn child can affect their lives for good or bad. Even though these children never made it into the world, they are still a part of the family lineage; therefore, they should be prayed for and given service or offerings so that they, too, can be at peace and ascend to their proper realm if they have not already.

Additionally, this subject is important because many people, such as I, have been told that we were cursed from birth. This curse could have been placed in any number of ways. It could have been generational; that is, it could have come from the energy of parents who did not want the child (which could have been for various unknown reasons). Family and/or friends who didn't want the birth to occur may have placed the curse. Or, lastly, the curse could have come from witchcraft. If you plan to have children, keep in mind the importance of being very aware of your feelings and emotions, as well as the feelings and emotions of others, while carrying your unborn child. Feelings and emotions are energies that can be transmitted and affect the child's spirituality from before birth. This energy could very well manifest later in the child's physical life, causing you, the parent, to pay through your child's growing years.

For instance, if either parent feels very strongly about not wanting a pregnancy that hasn't been planned, that energy can actually curse or cause the child great distress, on a spiritual level, as it develops in the womb. Then the child is plagued with negative circumstances throughout his or her life because the negative energy bestowed at birth has manifested into physical form. This happens even when other family members, such as grandparents, have negative thoughts about the child coming into the world. Remember, a child is always God's gift, and no matter how bad the circumstances may be at the time, try your best to maintain low stress levels. Be as positive, loving, and nurturing to your unborn child as you can, so, with good energy, you can increase your chances for having a happy and healthy baby, both physically and spiritually. Both parents (including same sex couples) can do something as simple as touching and praying over the mother's stomach as much as possible. Prayer is healing and is very powerful. It can make all the difference in the world, especially today. Children are in need of a lot of positive, prayerful energy, particularly with all the negative energies that they will encounter while growing up. For this reason, I have compiled a few prayers for our children that you may want to use:

Omnipotent God, I/we call upon the guardian spirits and protective angels in your holy name to watch over my/our child/ren, [name(s)]. We ask that he/she/they be protected in mind, body, and spirit. I/we ask that the power of God and the good spirits have a stronger influence over the actions of my/our child/ren than any negative influence of the visible or invisible worlds. Divine parent, you appointed the angels to take care of this/these child/ren, and therefore I/we ask that you not let any evil or bad spirits gain access to his/her/their mind(s). In the name of the most high, let [name(s)] resist all suggestions of evil on all levels of consciousness. Keep him/her/them safe and shielded from the dangers of the world, especially the hidden dangers, and let no weapons formed against him/her/them prosper. Thank you, good spirits and protective angels, for keeping your many promises of protection, and help him/ her/them walk in the ways of love, light, and goodness so that he/she/ they will forever remain under the umbrella of your holy protection. In the name of the most high, I pray. Amen.

PRAYER FOR UNBORN/ABORTED CHILD

Heavenly father/mother God, I call upon your mercy and compassion at this time. I ask that you hear my cry as I mourn the loss of my aborted child. I ask, dear Lord, that you take my child into your loving arms so that this soul will not suffer in the realm of spirit.

I know, father/mother God, that it may be selfish of me to ask, but I ask for your forgiveness and for the soul of my unborn not to suffer because of my actions. I fall onto bended knees and ask that this innocent child be surrounded by the holy angels and taken into the light of God.

Divine parent, I ask for help and that you give me the strength to place myself in better circumstances and that you give me the confidence to make better choices for myself in the future. Merciful God, I ask that in you I learn to love others and myself in the right way. Help me, father/mother God, to know true love with or without a mate so that I will not find myself in dire circumstances. I know that you are a forgiving God, and I ask for the strength to heal and forgive all others related to this situation and myself.

Above all, father/mother God, forgive me of all my sins, continue to watch over me, and protect me from the snare of my enemies. Keep the devil from my path, and let me not fall prey to negative suggestions. Watch over my friends and my loved ones, keeping us safe from harm. All this I ask in your glorious name. Amen.

Prayer for Unborn Miscarried/ Early Death

Mother/father God, I ask for your consolation in my/our time of mourning. Dear God, I ask that you and the good angels help me/us find the strength to heal, forgive, and love in my/our tragic moment.

Only you, God, know why my/our child was taken away from me/ us, but I trust in your decision, and I know that my/our child is safe with you. I ask, divine parent, that you take my/our child into your loving arms so that this soul will not suffer in the realm of spirit. I fall onto bended knees and ask that this innocent child be surrounded by the holy angels and taken into the light of God.

Merciful God, if there is a lesson that you are trying to teach me/us, give me/us the insight and strength to look past my/our grief to learn the lesson I am/we are supposed to learn. I pray that I/we can reaffirm my/our faith in you as the creator of all and that you will not let me/us down, nor will you let me/us fall.

All-powerful God, if my/our child's early death is the result of negative influences on any level, then Lord, I ask that you be my/our judge and jury in this matter. I ask that you protect me/us and keep me/us from the trenches of my/our enemies. Divine parent, I ask that you never let the consciousness of our enemies rest; however, please take the soul of my/our child into the light and give him/her his/her restful peace.

God of compassion, let your will be done and help me/us not to be bitter so that I/we can refocus my/our energy toward something positive, and may I/we continue to stand strong in the face of insurmountable odds for my/our family, as well as for myself/us. I ask this in the name of all that is holy, just, and pure in light and love. In the name of the most high, I pray.

TRADITIONAL NATIVE AMERICAN PRAYER

"O Great Spirit, whose voice I hear in the winds, and whose breath gives life to all the world; hear me, I come before you, one of your children.

I am small and weak. I need your strength and wisdom. Let me walk in beauty and make my eyes ever behold the red and purple sunset.

Make my hands respect the things you have made, my ears sharp to hear your voice.

Make me wise so that I may know the things you have taught my People.

The lessons you have hidden in every leaf and rock.

I seek strength not to be superior to my brothers, but to be able to fight my greatest enemy, myself.

Make me ever ready to come to you, with clean hands and straight eyes, so when life fades as a fading sunset, my spirit may come to you without shame."[3]

CHAPTER 11

DIVINATION

D ivination serves as a kind of road map to your life's path and even your destiny. It is the practice used to reveal accurate, hidden information or truth about the past, present, and future by psychic, or what are believed to be supernatural, means. Through the process of divination, people with special abilities—known as babalawos, diviners, mediums, priests, priestesses, psychics, santeros/santeras, shamans, or spiritists/spiritualists—interpret messages from various realms of the spirit world. They use their own type of oracle, source, or tool to help them reveal the mysteries of life.

From the Afrikan or Lukumi system, babalawos use the opon Ifa (divination tray) and/or the opele (sacred chain used for divining). Through this form of divination, Orunmila (god of wisdom and witness to God's creations) and Esu (god of justice and the messenger) collaborate to reveal to humans the secrets of the universe as well as the wishes of Olodumare (God) and the Òrìsà. The *merindinlogun* is a practice of casting 16 cowrie shells used by babalawos and initiated priests or priestesses within the Lukumi/Yoruban tradition. *Obi abata* (using sacred kolanut), which has four separable segments—two males and two females, representing the primary masculine and feminine forces of the universe—and *obi* (using four pieces of coconut) are used in divination by babalawos, initiates and non-initiates of this same system. Then there are numerous other systems, such as the oracle from the Egyptian/Kemetic system, the I-Ching, pendulums, tarot cards, astrology, numerology, mediums, and healers.

As with any system or medium of divination, the abilities, character, techniques, and experiences of the diviner make a huge difference in the validity of your reading. In my system of Lukumi/Yoruba, the opon Ifa and the merindinlogun (including obi abata and obi) are considered the most powerful and direct of all divination systems. Please keep in mind, though, that from system to system, different oracles can tap into different realms of spirit energy, and information can vary—or in some cases, come to the same conclusions—depending on the expertise of the diviner. All divination systems contain some value because all of them, in one way or another, hold the answers to issues relevant to human life, regardless of differences in national origin, creed, sex, religion, or culture. And whether one believes or not, these differences help us understand who we are, who others are, who the Creator is, and what our connections are to one another and to our universe.

So-called divinations and readings for entertainment purposes are one thing, but for the serious client, divination offers guidance and resolution to many pressing questions, particularly in the face of impossible circumstances. With so much at stake, it is important for a client to investigate the credibility of the diviner. Do not be afraid to ask questions, but at the same time, understand that the diviner may not be able to reveal everything—such as the secrets of their profession. Just know that you should feel some level of comfort regarding the answers. You should have an underlying feeling of recognition and confirmation, for on some level, you have known the truth all along.

Unfortunately, too many people have been deceived by psychics, priests and priestesses, witches, spiritualists, and shamans who claim to have special gifts and powers of prophecy when their main intentions were and are to misuse, abuse, and take advantage of the vulnerable. The reasons for deceit are primarily control and monetary gain. Credible and serious diviners, mediums, and spiritualists do not use their faculties in trivial or frivolous ways. They give the utmost sincere respect to their faculties and to the advice given to them from the realms of spirit. In their eyes, divination is a sacred tool. True diviners are professionals who have yielded to their destinies and surrendered themselves to the will of the universe, receiving energy and messages that will help them, their families, and their community as a whole.

Divining and mediumship are hard work, but to be considered a diviner or medium, one must have a connection to the spirit realm to ensure receipt of spiritual messages. It's the quality of the message that matters. Whatever the divination system used, it should form a bridge between the diviner and the higher realms to promote the delivery of healthy, constructive, and accurate messages and guidance— guidance being the key word. Many diviners or mediums have their own systems, structures, and disciplines regarding how they work, but overall, the interaction between the diviner and the client should be a professional, free-flowing, comfortable, and rewarding experience. Clients seeking assistance should be open-minded about the direction and advice given about their lives while knowing that they are in control to make their own decisions. However, there are diviners or mediums who misuse their faculties for control, harm, monetary gain, or instilling fear, just to become perpetrators of spiritual abuse. If you feel you are the victim of such a person, you should quickly seek help elsewhere.

One of the most important aspects of any divination system is interpretation. When interpreting messages and guiding people, the diviner or medium has to be as clear as possible, as well as responsible and intelligent enough to help the client understand their interpretations on a personal level—especially when the message can be taken either literally or figuratively. It is the diviner's responsibility to perfect his or her craft. In many circumstances this will require the diviner to continue to study, meditate, train, and practice in order to keep skills sharp. Continuing to study and train keeps the diviner in an elevated moral state of mind. Most clients have the tendency to take to heart what a diviner has said and will hold the diviner to his or her exact words, which can cause misunderstandings, the continuation of unhealthy relationships, break-ups in marriages or friendships, poor judgments, or poor decision-making. Therefore, it is highly important for a diviner to choose words carefully, and if a client does not understand something in a reading, he or she should definitely clarify his or her understanding before leaving the reading table or mat.

It is also helpful for a client to understand that the rules and processes for accessing information from the realm of spirit are different from system to system and from diviner to diviner. Many clients are unrealistic about what to expect from a diviner. Some clients think that diviners are psychic or available 24/7, can read minds, can give lotto numbers, can solve all their problems, are therapists, or can diagnose and cure illness. Although, under the right conditions, diviners of some spiritual systems (Ifa) can produce these results—but not in every instance because sometimes there are impeding circumstances. Also, in many cases and for various reasons, some clients are culprits of changing the meaning of the messages given to them, or they will process the information in a way that is damaging to their progress:

a client may be in denial, may have insecurities, may have been through traumatic situations, or may have a fear of losing something or someone of sentimental value. Or the client may change the meaning simply because the truth hurts. If you, the client, truly want guidance, it will benefit you to open yourself to the truth (of course, this assumes the information has been given to you in a constructive manner). For instance, if it is revealed through divination that your mate is cheating, this does not mean you should go home and try to harm that person, because clearly you will have a whole new set of negative circumstances to deal with if you react inappropriately. As hard as it may be, it just means that you will need to reevaluate your relationship to attempt to mend it, or find the strength to move on to a more positive situation, which in many cases may require some strategic planning.

Information is not revealed to you through the spirit realm to hurt you, even though the information itself may be hurtful. The elevated and intelligent spirits only tell you things that are going to help you and put you in a better position in life, and sometimes this shift is not pleasant. Working with spirit becomes important in the sense that it helps you make a conscious effort to take control of your life— whether it is purging negative energy or attracting positivity into your life. But above all, common sense should prevail, especially in delicate situations; so if your mate/partner is no good, accept that fact and, if possible, find a constructive way to let go and move onward. If your job is making you miserable, then get the strength to switch to something better, but don't leave your current job until you have something else lined up. A part of common sense is to plan and be strategic in your maneuvers in order to place yourself in the best possible situation. You don't want to create a whole new set of undesirable and unnecessary circumstances only because you do not have the patience to plan a way out. But if a situation needs to be accelerated, then you do what you gotta do. Thus, if any of us truly want guidance and help, we must trust and let go of all the things that hurt or stagnate us and cause drama in our lives.

Another very important aspect of divining is personal vs. spiritual advice. Anyone who has consulted a diviner has been a victim of receiving personal advice, whether intentionally or unintentionally. I am speaking of the use of personal advice in the negative sense, where diviners tell you what they, personally, believe to be true. This occurs because their views and perceptions have been jaded from within or from what they have heard from others. For instance, many diviners will tell you what *they* think you should do or not do about a particular situation and will give you prejudicial advice out of jealously, envy, narrow-mindedness, or what they think is helpful. These diviners fail to recognize that consultations/readings are not just spiritual but are also psychological, and that the information given can have a serious effect on the client's psyche—good or bad.

Please do not misunderstand. Personal advice can be wonderful, as long as the client clearly understands that this is what is being given, and that the advice is information in addition to, but separate from, the spiritual messages that were given in the reading. Personal advice is given for many reasons, usually out of caring and concern, but when a diviner purposely passes off personal advice as spiritual messages as a means to mislead or to have their own way, this should be considered unethical.

The beautiful thing about divination is that it can reveal many things—misfortunes/losses, illnesses and many other health problems, undesired circumstances, or destructive patterns that can develop in life. As well divination can reveal the blessings, goodness, wealth, prosperity, health, wellness, and children in your life. This is particularly true if you choose to have divination in the system of Lukumi/Yoruba. The diviner or medium can assess the situation at hand and, through a higher power, recommend how to deal with a positive or negative issue. Through this revelation, we get the opportunity to change our goals, focus, thinking, or even circumstances through what we call *ebbo* (a sacrifice) or an *adimu* (offering) to the higher powers and ancestors. On a high order, ebbo brings us into alignment with our destiny. Ebbo or adimu is given for many reasons. You can give an offering in sentiments to thank God, the Òrìsà, the ancestors, or your guides for all the blessings that they have bestowed upon you, or you can make sacrifices and give an offering to deter the progression of negative (energies) forces, conditions and circumstances. It is important to realize that conditions and circumstances can and do change. Sometimes the messages revealed through divination may stand true only for the present time or for a short period of time, which can sometimes be based on your current mode of thinking or how soon you take action regarding the impending circumstance. The whole purpose of divining is to find and possibly fix the problem or problems from the root. The process of healing or curing your circumstances starts with recognizing your own patterns of mental, emotional, or physical behaviors that may continue to obstruct your paths.

In many cases, clients and even initiates become fanatical and think that they can get around the truth or can gain quicker solutions by going to several different readers or diviners in search of answers or solutions that they feel will make them happy. Even in their state of impatience and avoidance, they soon come to find out, disappointingly, that the same messages continue to repeat themselves over and over again—no matter who does the divining. This will usually occur when the issue is of extreme importance and the spirit world is trying to make a point, or when the client continually chooses to ignore previous messages and is trying to hide from the truth.

Divination sessions, sacrifices, and offerings are all meant to facilitate and manipulate other energies to bring forth positive changes in our lives and to keep us on track with our destiny. Through divination itself, we ask the universal energies (the invisible realms of spirit) to visit us with news that will guide us, protect us, and heal us. We also ask them to bring along the appropriate ebbo, solution, or remedy (sacrifice or offering) that will stimulate and set the wheels in motion for the desired change. Ebbo is an act that helps us focus on maintaining and/or restoring our healthy states, whether emotional, mental, physical, or spiritual. Once we know what it is that we must do to initiate positive change, at that moment we must acknowledge the problems, take the necessary actions to submit and humble ourselves in sincere prayers, make the prescribed ebbo, and allow our intentions, the energies from within ourselves, and the ebbo to flow back into the universe to manifest, produce, alter, or bring forth new possibilities for our lives.

The ball is always in your court to take action, and all of us need to remember that we do have choices. It is up to us to take the initiative, to make the necessary changes that will better our lives. However, the future can be manipulated to a degree, and having created nature, God has the power to control and change the future and suspend or redirect nature's energies according to his will. So by making supplications and praying, we petition the Òrìsà, ancestors, and spirit guides to intervene between God and us so that any changes to our lives, on a spiritual level, will be beneficial to our personal and communal well- being.

On a final note, I must reiterate that common sense should rule over any divination system, particularly in the case of your health. If you are ill, you should seek a doctor immediately. Simply put, seek a doctor before divination and get more than one opinion, if necessary. Doctors are not infallible, either. If the doctor absolutely cannot find anything or is unable to help you, then seek divination to see if the illness is manifesting from the spiritual plane. If this is the case, an ebbo or adimu (offering) is divined for, prescribed and supplicated to the spirits to possibly alleviate the problem.

CHAPTER 12

WHAT'S NEXT?

Aside from connecting with your ancestors and spirit guides/eguns, finding good guidance to further your exploration or initiation into Ifa, Lukumi/Yoruba, or similar systems like Candomblé, Vodoun, or Palo Mayombe is not an easy task. Where you go from here really depends on what road you would like to take and how far you want to go. Do you just want to delve into spiritualism on an informal basis for yourself and your family? Do you want to be associated with a spiritual group where you can learn and grow, eventually becoming qualified to help others? Or do you want to continue your spiritual studies toward initiation and priesthood?

The attractive thing about connecting with your ancestors and spirit guides/eguns is that you do not need initiation, nor do you need to belong to any kind of religious or spiritual group. But there are societies of Òrìsà veneration, ancestor worship, and egun/spirit reverence that do require initiation by way of ceremony, such as Ifa, Lukumi/Yoruba, Candomblé, Vodoun, Mayombe, the Egungun, and the Gelede societies, just to name a few. However, I can only speak on behalf of Lukumi/Yoruba and

Palo Mayombe systems, for I have been initiated into both. If you are interested in spiritual systems other than Lukumi/Yoruba or Palo Mayombe, I am certain that you will still be able to take into consideration many of my suggestions and apply them to your situation and spiritual path of choice, for all of the systems mentioned are similar in many ways.

For those of you who are at the point where you want to take your devotion to the next level toward priesthood, then you are now considered an aleyo in the Lukumi system. An aleyo is Lukumi terminology to mean an individual who is considered an outsider to an Òrìsà-based community because he or she has not been initiated into priesthood, but aspires to practice the traditions of Lukumi/Yoruba. Once initiated into the traditions of Lukumi/Yoruba as a priest or priestess, you are titled Olorìsà. As an Olorìsà, Òrìsà priest, you will have certain rights and the license to work, perform, and/or attend divination sessions, rituals, and ceremonies. However, until you become an Olorìsà, and while you are still in the beginning stages of devotion, there are three words and concepts—community, culture, and tradition—that you, the aleyo, must first understand and adhere to, as these words are the foundation upon which Lukumi/Yoruba stands.

The New Webster's Comprehensive Dictionary defines **community** as (1) a body of people with a faith, profession or way of life in common; (2) a body of people living near one another as in a village community; (3) a sharing of interest. **Culture** is defined as (1) the training and development of the mind; (2) the social and religious structures and intellectual and artistic manifestations, etc. that characterize a society. **Tradition** is defined as (1) a cultural continuity transmitted in the form of social attitudes, beliefs, principles, and conventions of behavior deriving from past experience and helping to shape the future; (2) a religious law or teaching, or a body of these, held to have been received originally by oral transmission.

Therefore, Lukumi/Yoruba is a community-based traditional religious system, meaning that the Òrìsà community is a body of individuals who live in close proximity to one another and who believe and share common interests and spiritual/religious beliefs. Lukumi/Yoruba is based on a modified tribal and cultural structure (a community that preserves its own customs, beliefs, and organization without interference from outside communities and customs) passed on from the ancestors. This includes chains of command, the allocation of functions between priests and non-priests, levels of hierarchy (specification of rank/titles), and unity of purpose. Everything is structured to ensure some sort of central order and synchronized action within the community.

As a result, if you want to participate you will be expected to follow the norms of an Òrìsà-based community; you will need the ability to adapt and change your current way of being to fit in; and you will be expected to function within the community open-mindedly and as a team player and embrace Cuban/Yoruban culture, including its traditions, history, arts, clothing, and language. For some this is easier said than done, particularly for those whose views and patterns of living are Amerikanized. It is sometimes more difficult for Amerikans to adapt to Afrikan-based customs, because many live with more individualistic thought patterns (the "everyone for self" mentality) than communal ideology. Amerikan morals, values, and belief systems are based on Anglo and European customs, and it is very hard for many Amerikan-born individuals to embrace alternative customs. This is particularly true for those whose distant heritage is Afrikan-based; when these individuals are placed in situations that require them to acknowledge their distant heritage, they feel uncomfortable or uneasy, and it becomes a struggle on many levels, both conscious and subconscious, because they cannot relate. It is sad, because most people of color can readily and easily accept the concept of Jesus being white, but they are embarrassed to be associated with a rich Afrikan lineage of kings, queens, and noblemen and women who have also elevated to sainthood or godship—these are the Black gods and goddesses who looked like us, people with pigmented skin. It is disheartening that in the eyes of some, Black faces have no place in heaven, nor could they hold the role of a deity or a god. It is even more heartbreaking that most people cannot even conceptualize or picture a god of pigmented skin, and if you are known to worship such a god, you are considered to be in the employ of Satan.

This is not about racism or segregation. This is about knowing and opening your mind to all the possibilities that the deities, gods and goddesses, saints, angels, and even spirits come in all colors (or are without color or gender) and are all agents of "The One—The Creator" in one way or another. These agents are placed at various locations around the world, all with the authority and the responsibility of adjudicating and intervening in the affairs of heaven and earth. Moreover, no religious system—Afrikan, Asian, Christianity, Islam, Judaism, etc.—or godhead of that system can claim to be "The Only and the Right One" because God specifically created them all to help manage the planetary system. Each godhead dignitary, whether Orunmila, Òrìsà, Christ, Buddah, Muhammad, archangels, ascended masters, or others, as agents of God, came to various parts of the world to assist the forces of good in dominating the forces of evil and to make the world a more livable and enlightened place for humans. The common denominator between all of them is that they inspire their followers not to do any evil or destroy their fellow beings, because it is against nature to do so.

The only way to understand and embrace other cultures, including Òrìsà culture, is to see it, breathe it, taste it, feel it, live it, or experience it in some way. And for those who live in the United States and are interested in the Lukumi/Yoruba religious system, the need to modify Western, European, or Amerikanized ways of thinking and being are essential. Therefore, if you are the type of person who is not used to community-based or family-oriented settings, or if you are the type of person who is difficult to get along with, a loner, or a non-team player, or if you have individualistic ideals, then you will certainly have difficulty adjusting to the protocols associated with this spiritual system. As an aleyo on the road to becoming an olorìsà, Òrìsà priest or priestess, you will be required to accept and adhere to many rules and regulations, standards and ethics, moral codes, taboos, and responsibilities, along with many other expectations, such as respect, humility, patience, and sacrifice.

The only way to become an olorìsà, Òrìsà priest is to be initiated through a ceremony called kari-ocha, or ocha. Most compare ocha to a marriage between the initiate and their guardian Òrìsà (this guardian Òrìsà or divinity is the one that was assigned to govern over this person at birth). This ceremony of ocha is much deeper than the union between a man and a woman because there is no such thing as separation or divorce, and it is something that stays with you for your entire life and afterward. Once this ceremony is done to you, whether you stay with it, walk away, or get rid of all your sacred items and belongings, it remains with you forever, even in the afterlife. In metaphysical terms, ocha would be energy of varying degrees from within the universe (nature) that influences your being and your soul on a spiritual level, in turn rearranging, adjusting, or fixing your physical being. Your life, your personality, your character, and your behavior are shaped by all kinds of experiences in the physical world; however, ocha is about evolution and growth, whether animate or inanimate, seen or unseen, mild or drastic. Ocha is a state of mind in the highest regard, and the purpose of such an initiation is to bring you in alignment with your destiny. Ocha is an ever-present energy that never dies, and it is how you learn to understand and interpret life on the physical, mental, emotional, and spiritual planes.

Learning to understand nature and the universe is how you can learn to understand yourself as well as the Òrìsà. Remember, Òrìsà are the Afrikan gods that rule the natural forces within the universe. For instance, the ocean waters are ruled by Yemaya and Olokun, the wind is ruled by Oya, and volcanic activity is ruled by Aganju. Through Òrìsà reverence, we learn about Olodumare (God) and God within, about Òrìsà (nature) and Òrìsà within, and about the universe and the universe within ourselves. So, taking all of this into consideration, kari-ocha can be viewed as a science and philosophy that teaches us about life and the principles of all existence. It is a life-altering event, both physically and spiritually, that should not be taken lightly. However, there are those who take an insecure, haphazard, and nonchalant attitude towards ocha, and sadly, they miss out on the real philosophy and true meaning of what Òrìsà reverence stands for. Another unfortunate fact is that many priests and non-priests alike diminish the characteristics, powers, and abilities of the Òrìsà to human tendencies; the Òrìsà are belittled to human standards and are treated with little dignity.

In my opinion, when we think of the Òrìsà, we must try not to compare them to humans, even though they were once considered such. The fact that we as humans use only a very small percentage of our brains lets you know how debilitated, limited, and crippled we really are. We have so many limitations that to compare or bring Òrìsà down to a human level truly is a discredit to them. However, the one great aspect about Òrìsà is that they are non-discriminatory. They will love you, protect you, deal with you, and work with you no matter who you are, what level you are, or what your place in society is, as long as you remain respectful; and even when some people aren't totally respectful, many (not all) of the Òrìsà will maintain a high level of tolerance with warnings that these people must change their disrespectful behaviors or suffer dire consequences. Just know and remember that the powers of Òrìsà are endless, and the possibilities for change in our lives are infinite. The only limitations will come from you.

Many walk into this religion with the mistaken idea and expectation that change should be instantaneous or painless, and when outcomes do not manifest at the drop of a dime, everything gets written off as a failure, including, at times, the religion as a whole. People are so dependent and codependent on everything and anything else to save them that they forget change happens only with the *assistance* of our guides in the spirit realm and within the universe. It is not the sole responsibility of the universe to save us. It is up to us to learn how to use the tools, such as divination, rituals, offerings, and solutions, given to us from God, the Òrìsà, our ancestors, spirit guides, and spirit teachers to help us grow and become co-creators of our destinies.

Many of you reading this book are already familiar with Òrìsà and ancestor and spirit/egun veneration. Your familiarity may come from reading books, from family and/or friend involvement, from personal experience, or from the guidance of a godparent/elder, or you may be associated with an ile (house of Òrìsà and ancestor veneration) that provides teachings and guidance on a formal or informal basis. If this describes you, then you already have a wonderful start. Unfortunately, for those who would love to delve deeper into the mysteries but have no clue where to go from here, you have reached the hard part. In moving forward and deciding the next step for yourself, you will need to determine which path you want to take. Some of you will know immediately, while others will have a clearer picture as time moves forward. However, before moving forward, I would like to mention a few things from my experiences and point of view that you should keep in mind. They may help you decide where to begin.

If you are at the point where you prefer to work alone without any kind of godparent influence, then at a minimum I recommend you hire a spiritualist/medium who is a group leader to other spiritualists/ mediums who can conduct a spiritual session called a misa/séance— or in the Spanish community, a white table mass—preferably in your own home. If it is not feasible for you to have a misa/séance or white table mass in your home, then the head spiritualist will probably recommend that it be done in their home instead. It is the job of the spiritualist and/or medium to investigate, analyze, and produce facts from the spirit realm about the happenings in your life and to provide solutions to any pending issues you may have.

Provided that you have chosen competent and experienced mediums, conducting a misa/séance or white table mass will prove very beneficial to you. At a minimum, you will get the opportunity to know how your ancestors and spirit guides/eguns feel about the status of your life or if there is negativity affecting you. The spiritualist will provide you with the opportunity to clean up your spirit realm, ridding yourself and your home of unwanted spirit entities.

Depending on the depth of your spiritual realm (how many spirits are influencing your life for good or bad), you may need more than one spiritual session. This provides you with the perfect opportunity to sort through some confusing or troublesome issues, plus you get to find out details on who your ancestors and spirit guides/eguns are and their purposes in your life. This is also where your spirit guides get very specific about what kinds of changes need to occur in your life for your well-being, and how they would like you to work and take care of them for your combined progression. In addition, there are many psychics who work on an individual basis who are gifted at identifying spirit guides and spirit teachers, but keep in mind to choose someone who is familiar with your cultural needs.

***It is important to note that you must do your research on individuals who claim to be mediums, psychics, or spiritists/ spiritualists. Word of mouth is your best bet, and the best advice I can offer is that you get as many referrals as you can that will make you feel comfortable before inviting anyone into your home. Always think about safety and beware of con artists. If it is possible, ask if you can be invited to a couple of spiritual sessions that are being done for someone else. This way you can feel out the person first. If you are not comfortable, do not rush into anything. You don't have to feel pressured, because at the very least, you can continue to pray on your own about your situation, and in your prayers you can ask your spirit guides/ eguns to bring good and competent people into your life to help you. Trust me — your spirit guides/eguns will understand that you just want to be cautious. If you have a spirit guide that is not cooperative or understanding, then this guide is inferior and not enlightened. You need to know that no guide should place you in a dangerous situation. Take your time, because rushing without caution can make a bad situation worse. If you do not have competent individuals at your disposal to help you spiritually, then your guides will need to be just as patient as you are until the right person and situation presents itself.

If spiritualism and mediumship is your chosen passion and you would like to work as a medium, then you will need a spiritual godparent or teacher, or you will need to join a spiritual group of experienced professionals skilled in this area, so that you can properly and safely get the knowledge necessary to grow and become qualified to help others. Whether you are part of a group or have an elder/ teacher training you, there are several things that should be done. (1) At a minimum, your ancestors and spirit guides/eguns should be identified so that you will know which guides are assisting you with your development. (2) If you do not have an altar or shrine set up in your home, you may want to set one up; this will be your focal point and the place where you can communicate and work with your spirit guides/eguns on a continuous basis. However, this is not always necessary. Some individuals and spiritualists can work with the spirit realms extremely well without an altar. (3) Your elder or group should be able to give you some information on what is needed to appease your spirit guides/eguns. (4) And lastly, your elder or group of mediums should be able to investigate stagnant areas of your life and offer solutions to clean up and/or better your life.

***It is not necessary to know the names of your ancestors or spirit guides/eguns. It is helpful, but not necessary. If needed, you can give them names that you choose. Our ancestors and spirit guides/ eguns love us and care for us no matter what. It is enough for them to know that you are at least attempting to acknowledge and develop long-standing relationships with them.

For some of you, your path may end here. If it does, I wish you all the best; may God and the good spirits accompany you always in light, peace, and harmony. But if you have opted to move onward into priesthood and, as mentioned previously, as an aleyo, you will need to take the following into consideration.

Involvement in this religion will require you to live Lukumi/ Yoruba as a way of life. It is not a game or a fad. This is not the kind of spiritual system that you can just pick up and put down anytime you like. Unlike many other religions and spiritual systems, the Lukumi/Yoruban system provides specific instructions and solutions for every issue in life, and the messages and divinations that are given to each individual are unique. It would make perfect sense that the messages given to us from the spirit realms would be individualized person-to-person, because every person has a different path. Divination is how the Òrìsà, ancestors, and spirits guide us down our chosen path.

Lukumi/Yoruba is a hands-on spiritual system, and you will become a part of a community that is based on customs and tribal structures, both Cuban and Yoruban. Participation is crucial to your phases of growth; not only do you grow in faith, but you will also grow in spirit by using your physical, mental, and emotional involvement in rituals and ceremonies, especially if you're initiated. Even if you are not yet initiated, participation is just as crucial because there are so, so many things that can be learned outside of the actual ritual and ceremony. Learning can be enhanced by hearing the stories and conversations from elders, watching the preparation of ingredients—particularly working herbs for rituals and ceremonies, working in the kitchen, and running errands (very important duties within this system because you get to see and learn what ingredients and groceries are needed to make successful rituals and ceremonies). These are the types of things that you can only discover hands-on and by repetition.

Keep in mind that the road toward priesthood can be very short (months) for some and very long (years) for others. Everyone has his or her time. Some individuals will need to be initiated immediately for emergency reasons, such as illness, while others have a choice to be initiated, even though initiation may not be necessary for them. Lukumi/Yoruba is one system that accepts all, regardless of gender, color, race, ethnicity, creed, or religious status although there is continued controversy over gay men becoming babalawos. Some will develop and grow quickly, while others may do it more slowly. In many instances, this is the natural progression of how the Òrìsà's energy is working with you, but it could also depend on how much effort and work you put in yourself. Some people float effortlessly through this system while others have to work their fingers to the bone, because, for whatever reason, the Òrìsà want these people to savor and appreciate what they have had to work hard for. When many people get things too easily, they do not appreciate what they have. The process towards priesthood and beyond will be different for everyone, and there are many, many reasons why people gravitate towards this spiritual/religious system.

Everything is a process, and the secrets of this system must be *earned*. They are not given to you on a silver platter. If you think about it, this is true no matter what type of system you may decide to delve into, whether it is Buddhism, college, karate, Lukumi/Yoruba, Freemasonry, meditation, mediumship, Palo, sororities/fraternities, spiritualism, Wicca, yoga, etc. All of these systems have varying degrees of discipline, information, exercise, sacrifice, and work that must be mastered before you can even think about reaching the next level. Even something like losing weight requires all of the things that I just mentioned. For certain people, these uncomfortable aspects are very necessary in preparing you and helping you acquire better character and maintaining a steady and stable state of mind. Everyone must crawl before they walk, and the new jacks must pay their dues—not just to gain access to higher levels but to gain the respect of others, as well. As in any spiritual system or with anything acquired in life that is deemed worthwhile, *determination*, *hard work*, and some sort of *sacrifice* are required in order for you to reach your goals of elevation.

Understand that any reputable system that is protective and takes pride in its beliefs will have firewalls in place, and the only way to get through these firewalls is to *earn* passage. Whether you are an initiate or non-initiate, you have to *earn* your way. That may mean beading, sewing, cleaning, cooking, and working in the kitchen, which could include plucking, listening and not talking, having patience, sitting in silence, studying, saluting your elders numerous times, or sacrificing time and money. This is all a part of the process. Know that even the most trivial, brainless, and boring chores that are done in this religion have a purpose and set the foundation for effective rituals and ceremonies. Even the smallest of chores cannot be skipped over or left out, because this could affect the outcome of an entire ceremony. Shortcuts are no good in this religion. Therefore, lots of patience is required, and not everything is going to be fun. Sometimes we have to go through tons of what we think are long, drawn-out prayers, but they are important in the elevation of our spirituality and to place us on our correct path. These are the steps and tests necessary to pass in order to make the grade and move on to the next level. This is another reason why physical participation and hands-on experience is important. The step-by-step details, the prayers, the songs, the ingredients, and the smallest of actions used to activate and give power to the rituals and ceremonies will not be found in books or on the Internet.

The connection between you and your spiritual family/community and the invisible realm gains strength by your physical presence. I feel for those of you who live great distances from any Òrìsà community, because the need to have access to other olorìsàs, priests, and priestesses is very important for your development and growth process. It is not enough to be initiated, except in the case where it is divined that an individual is not to participate in ceremony and/or rituals. You have to have accessibility to other priests in order to learn, work, and put into practice the teachings and traditions of Òrìsà reverence, especially since the majority of information is given orally and the rituals and ceremonies are done in group or community settings, usually with an elder or elders supervising the process. Therefore, the only way to learn these things, as repeatedly stated, is to physically participate and to see and learn with your own eyes. And while learning, keep in mind that you should also maintain some level of patience; don't give in to your curiosity or desire to learn too much, too quickly. Many feel rushed to learn and absorb tons of information, and while that is commendable in some cases, too much information before it is time to learn it can be damaging. One reason it can be damaging is that many like to take information and run with it by doing things to or for themselves or others without understanding the full ramifications if things are not done correctly or completely. Consequently, they put themselves or someone else in jeopardy. In the spiritual systems for which we are practicing, Lukumi/Yoruba or even Palo, all lessons, information, and rituals must be disseminated in moderation and learned in completion. It can be disastrous to jump ahead. When unsure, even the most experienced priest and priestess will seek out elder advice on matters in question. The secrets of these systems are sacred and should be handled with the utmost respect and care.

This does not mean that you cannot take an assertive approach to learning; it just means that you have to maintain some level of patience, because not all the information for learning will be as readily accessible in the way you would like it to be. There are many reasons for this. For one, many elders hold back information because they have made tremendous strides and sacrifices to acquire their obtained level of knowledge, and they do not want to be frivolous in giving it away. Two, many priests have had plenty of bad experiences with clients, aleyos, and new initiates, and they do not want to give valuable information to those who may be non-appreciative or may use that information for all the wrong reasons. And because of the experiences and/or struggles that many priests and priestesses have had to endure, you will find that some priests have a strict, stern, outspoken, and painfully blunt demeanor. They do not play games. Do not be alarmed or take it personally. Just understand that it is not easy to deal with the public, and many priests and priestesses are sincere yet serious about their beliefs. They hold Òrìsà, the ancestors, and spirit guides/eguns in very high regard. Their oath is to protect and uphold tradition, not to cater to people who whimper or spiritual and religious abusers. Lastly, many seek Lukumi/Yoruba for many superficial reasons and/or to satisfy some kind of power fix. These individuals realize too late that bad and rash actions have many consequences. Abusers of the tradition of initiation do not comprehend that there is a great deal of responsibility that comes along with obtaining and maintaining power on any level.

If you are following the road of priesthood, the next recommendation for you as an aleyo—a non-initiated/non-ordained priest—is to find an ile (house of Òrìsà reverence) and a godparent to represent and take care of you in your developmental phases. It is worth noting that not all iles/houses work the same. The basic structure is the same, but the rules may vary from ile to ile (house to house). For instance, some iles/houses do not delve into spiritualism at all, and this works for them. This is their house rule and this is what their godchildren and clients will follow. It is the responsibility of your godparent and/or ile to guide you through all the necessary steps toward priesthood if this is your chosen path. It would be beneficial for you to familiarize yourself with the following common types of godparents:

Godparent A: These individuals specialize in spiritualism and mediumship. Some of them are initiated priests or priestesses; however, there are many who only practice as spiritualists/spiritists and mediums, and that is all they do. They are experts at spirit communication on many levels, and they usually divine while in trance/spirit possession or by using tools such as tarot cards, crystal balls, water, shells, stones, bones, etc. They also work their energies and their spirit guides through special rituals and offerings, and they specialize in healing baths, floor washes, and candle work using oils and herbs. Individuals who are only spiritists and mediums and are not initiates of Òrìsà priesthood cannot fully represent you on your journey to priesthood, not because they could not serve a genuine purpose, but because they lack initiation themselves and could only take you so far.

Many come to seek the road to Òrìsà priesthood through spiritists and mediums, and it is very common for priests and priestesses who are godparents to pay for the services of or take their godchildren to others in the community who specialize in spiritualism/mediumship just because this is their realm of expertise.

Godparent B: These individuals are initiates of Palo Mayombe or Palo Monte and are called paleros or paleras. "Within Palo, there are several types of branches that use different elder systems. Initiates from the Briyumberos or Kimbiseros branches that derived from the areas of Havana, Cuba, use an elder hierarchical system of tata/padrino/father and yaya/madrina/mother distinctions. The hierarchical system of the Casamundo branch or branches around the Camaguey Orient distinguish their elders by elder brother/ sister or younger brother/sister, which is kanda/clan/tribe based with the bambuta or elders leading the show. Then you have Palo Haitiano and some Mayombe branches, from the eastern Cuba region, that have a hierarchical system set up as a tierra or potencia, which is a council of elders called mfumus. They assist in running the casamundo that is under an elder's trunk/tronko (lineage) and an elder's supervision. They distinguish their members as elder brother/sister or younger brother/sister, which are also kanda/clan/ tribe based with elders leading the show.

There are seven Kongo-derived lines or lineages and numerous branches: (1) Mayombe, (2) Briyumba, (3) Viyumba, (4) Kimbisa, (5) Malongo, (6) Shamalongo, and (7) Palo Haitiano. Many have treaties with one another, and they interchange customs by crossing staffs. Each line has its own way of doing Palo, yet they can cross over, such as Mayombe with Briyumba, or Viyumba with Kimbisa. Each collective agreement is between the living and the dead of one house. You may find variance even in how the lines operate, because some have heavy Òrìsà influence while others are traditional Kongo and do not mix with any other traditions or religions. There are even some lines that have Christian influence because the Catholic Church has been in the Kongo since the 1490s, and many of the Kongo noblemen were Catholic; they just did things in the Kongo way instead of the Roman way."[7] Palo is a belief system that centers on the forces of nature. The practice and veneration of Palo deals with consecrated "pots" that are commonly known as prendas or nganga. These prendas or nganga are consecrated with particular prayers, songs, sticks, bones, dirt, and herbs that are sacred to a particular spirit of Palo and are only given to individuals who have gone through all the proper ceremonies. These spirits are called Nfumbes or Bakulu (ancestors) in other branches that are of much importance to the paleros. Paleros work these spirits and gain their assistance for reading people, helping and healing people, protecting themselves or others within the family line, and helping all others designated to follow this road.

It is important to note that this form of reverence is totally distinct, separate, and different from Òrìsà reverence and practice. Even though many attempt to compare Palo veneration to Òrìsà reverence, mainly because they both center on the forces of nature, you must understand that they are by no means the same. One system has nothing at all to do with the other. If an individual is initiated into both systems, they should not mix or mingle the two in any way, form, or fashion, and if they do, this practice is not traditional Lukumi/Yoruba, nor is it acceptable.

Palo initiates are devotees of the Kongo/Bantu system. Many of you will have a calling to practice this system, but understand that Palo is a very misunderstood system and, unfortunately, it has a bad name. This is because Kongo (Palo) spirits can work for good or bad, but most individuals choose to use them for bad. Despite what you might hear, I believe that Kongo spirits have the reputation for being inferior only because the majority of the individuals who use Palo energy are inferior in mind, heart, and spirit. Spirits can be elevated and educated as long as there are educated, good-hearted, and great people who prefer to work Palo as a means for saving souls and pulling positive energy that is meant to bring about long-term, positive effects on people's lives. Everyone has their own view and motives for why they choose to become initiated into the mysteries of Palo, whether good or bad, but I think that working evil is by choice. I believe that we learn from our spirits (Palo or otherwise), and they learn from us as well. It is not the gun that is dangerous, but the person who holds it! Yes, Palo eguns have the ability to work positive and negative, but the person who holds that energy in their hands makes the choice.

People are attracted to Palo because of its power and quick effectiveness, but Palo, if not used or taught properly, can destroy even its owner. Many do not realize that when Palo energy is used for bad purposes, its power has the potential to come back to haunt, hurt, or even kill them. Palo works and uses the forces of nature and the universe; if you use it for bad,

bad will come back around full circle to hit you. If you have a calling for this path, you must research and make sure that you find the right Palo house that upholds and believes in the same ethics and standards that you do. Palo is definitely not for everyone, and old-fashioned Palo houses are very, very strict. At the same time, a good house should teach excellent character and inspire education; health consciousness; mental, emotional, and financial prosperity; and healing to all those who need it. A Palo house should also teach control of emotions and positivity in thoughts and actions. Lastly, it is very common to find that initiates of this system can also be priests and priestesses of Òrìsà, as with Godparent A.

Godparent C: These individuals are initiated as priests or priestesses in the Afrikan diaspora (Lukumi/Yoruba system), also known as olorìsà, babalochas, and iyalochas, or santeros and santeras. They are priests of Òrìsà/nature reverence. If you are seeking priesthood, you will definitely need a competent godparent from this category to represent you. They will be able to guide you through all the proper steps towards priesthood, including all those previously mentioned.

Godparent D: These godparents, called babalawos or oluwos, are male priests who have been initiated into the mysteries of Ifa. Ifa is invocation, divination, notation, and interpretation, which brings forth resolution. In general terms, babalawos are priests of the Òrìsà Orunmila, the divinity of divination and witness to the creation of earth and of man. The babalawo, the father and keeper of Ifa secrets, divines and interprets the oracle of Ifa. To practice Ifa, is to practice a way of life. Ifa means to scrap, scrub/scratch, and swallow. This meaning comes from the story of how Olodumare gave Orunmila 16 kegs of wisdom to swallow. However, one of the kegs dropped and broke. Orunmila then began to pick up and swallow the shattered pieces of knowledge; the residual had to be scrapped from the ground. When the other Òrìsàs heard this, they were disappointed to have missed out, but none the less, they scrubbed and scratched what they could from the ground where the broken pieces fell and swallowed what wisdom they could because by doing so, they felt that they, too, had shared the wisdom with Orunmila. Ifa is the "word, wisdom, and coded messages" of Olodumare (God) that was made available to humankind by Orunmila, and it was foretold that through Ifa, every problem known to man can be resolved.

Godparent E: These godparents come from other Afrikan-based spiritual systems such as Haitian Vodou, Sanse, and Dominican Vodou known as 21 Divisions. These systems are popular but are not as well known as Santeria or Lukumi/Yoruba in the United States. Information about these spiritual systems are very limited. However, I thought that if any of you are interested in this path, it would be worthwhile to mention them. Houngan Hector, who is a priest and elder of all three systems mentioned, contributed the following text (see the bibliography for more information).

HAITIAN VODOU OVERVIEW

Although there are many initiate rankings/levels under this particular spiritual system and tradition, godparents/elders under this system are usually called Mambo (female) or Houngan (male). Initiates under this system work with spirits/egun called *"lwa"* or *"loa"* who are considered the "angels" of Vodou. Lwa means "law" referring to the law and principles within nature. To work with the "lwa" is to know and follow nature's laws. In this system God is most often seen as distant and not readily accessible to humans because the Creator is considered too busy. Due to this, God has invested power in these spirits known as the Lwa who are meant to serve the human as the human serves them. Aspirants of this system are called vodouisants and they do not worship the lwa. Instead, the lwa are served by the giving of their favorite foods, the wearing of their colors, the observance of their sacred days with abstinence, and participating in Vodou ceremonies, etc. It is believed that without human the Lwa would not exist, and without them we would cease to exist as well.

The vodou liturgy is divided into three separate groups. The first of these is Rada. The majority of the Rada Lwa come from Dahomey. Dahomey is now known as Benin. Some lwa that come from Dahomey are Danbala Wedo, Ayida Wedo, Sobo, etc. They are spirits that traveled from Africa over to Haiti. The Rada lwa are considered to be cool, stable, and beneficent. They are associated with the color white. Their stance is more defensive than aggressive.

At the end of the Rada liturgy, you have the service of other Lwa from different areas of Africa, most notably Ogou. The Ogou lwa are much more like a family of similar spirits, they are the spirits of the Nago Nation. In fact they are more frequently referred as belonging to the Nago nasyon (nation) rather than a family. They came from Nigeria. In this nation you have spirits such as Ogou Shango, Ogou Batala, Ogou Badagri, Ossanj, etc. These lwa have their own drum beats, their own protocol, and their own ritual.

Then you have the Petro Lwa. Petro Lwa are associated with the color red. They are considered more aggressive, fierce in fact, faster to act against enemies, and particularly effective in the quickness of their magick. The real differentiation of the Lwa Rada and Petro is their origin. Petro Lwa tend to be Kongo, Kreyol spirits, or in fact from a number of different African tribes. Within the Petro rite, we have many other nasyon. Examples of these are the Ibo, Wangol, and Kongo. The origins of the Petro Lwa are also more obscure. Right in there with the Petro lwa, you have the Lwa Marinette who was once a living person. She conducted the ceremony at Bwa Kayman to Ezili Danto, sacrificing a black female pig, thus marking the beginning of the Haitian Revolution.

You also have the Gede lwa. They are seen as a family, with Baron and Brijit. The Lwas Baron and Brijit bring about the rebirth of the spirits of the deceased, who then become Gede Lwa. They are countless; being that they are constantly being rebirthed giving rise to so many Gede lwa. There are also some Gede lwa that are "rasin" (have root aspects). One of these is Brav Gede Nibo, often seen as the first ancestor.

SANSE OVERVIEW

Sanse is a tradition of Spiritism that is mixed with other influences. In this tradition, Haitian and Dominican Vodou are mixed with Espiritismo de La Mesa Blanca. This tradition is geared towards elevating all of the spiritual tableaus and frameworks that an individual may have with him or her. A spirit is a body of energy that is supposed to evolve in order to become better. You are a spirit, encased in a body. A spiritual tableau or framework are various and distinct spirits that become close to a person. Initiation into Sanse speeds up the spiritual evolution of the individual. It also assists in making that person a better medium for their spiritual tableau and framework. Also, initiation removes certain types of spirits which cause the medium to be held back from his or her further evolution.

Sanse is different from *Mesa Blanca* in that it also deals with Loas or Misterios, as they are known. There are various forms of these spirits known in different parts of the world, such as in the Dominican Republic, Haiti, and Africa. Within Sanse, a variety of new Loa (Lwa) show up. They are very quick to apply solutions, much faster than other spirits. The initiation into Sanse is a process in which one starts to receive communication and instruction from these entities. These entities come to reinforce and give power to the spiritual tableau and framework of an individual. Thus these ceremonies are much more complicated than Mesa Blanca Spiritism.

In Sanse, other than the initiation, the initiator is there for the initiate only, to guide the individual when they become confused about something that their spiritual tableau and framework may have asked them to do. Since the Spirits teach directly, very little is needed from the initiator except for the initiation itself.

DOMINICAN VODOU
21 DIVISIONS OVERVIEW

Many are confused between *Sanse* and *Dominican Vodou* and think them to be the same. They are not. Although the Sancista (initiate of Sanse as mentioned above) does work with many of the spirits that are served within Dominican Vodou, it is not the same tradition and it is a different form of working with the spirits. Some will say that Dominican Vodou is Haitian Vodou, just practiced in the Dominican Republic. This is not true. Although there are many similar Lwa in Dominican Vodou, services and ceremonies are done differently. And the many different types Lwa are worked or served in a different manner than in Haiti.

In Dominican Vodou, God and the Virgin Mary are referred to often and many make petitions to them. There are Lwa within the tradition as well. Many times Dominican

Vodou is also called *The 21 Divisions*. In Dominican Vodou, one receives initiations but they serve a different purpose than in Haitian Vodou. In Dominican Vodou, initiation is a ceremony that aligns the individual to their spirits and gives them *"fuerza"* or power. It empowers them to work with their Lwa but an uninitiated individual can do so as well. These ceremonies serve to give the individual a firmer (stronger) and more stable foundation when working with their spirits. There are three different initiations that one may receive in this tradition.

This spiritual system and tradition is similar to Sanse, in that the Lwa teach their children how to do many different things. But there are some traditions and rules in Dominican Vodou that differ from Sanse, and there are some very definite ways to do certain things like how and what to service the Lwa is taught to the new initiate, although this information is *not* hard to find. Certain other rules are also followed and this tradition does not have as many rules as Haitian Vodou.

Dominican Vodou practitioners are often called *"Caballos"* but they are also known as *Papa Bokos* and *Papa Lwa* (both for males) and *Mama Mambos* and *Mama Lwa* (both for females). One who has obtained this title has gone through the last and highest level of initiation that can take anywhere between 3 to 9 days and nights. This spiritual system is usually for individuals who are called (or has a calling) to it. Some people are called at an earlier age than others and thus are able to develop within the tradition at a faster and more advanced rate.

Take care and do research to find competent godparents/elders within all religious/spiritual systems. Unfortunately, many so-called priests and priestesses are not appropriately initiating people into these mysteries. For instance, an initiation that should take several days is being done in as little as two hours! And in addition to some ceremonies being performed incorrectly, the wrong tools and sacred items are being given. These situations are scandalous and evil, to say the least. Then, when it is time for the new initiate to begin, that person is confused and at a complete loss.

Remember, just because an individual, priest, or priestess appears knowledgeable does not mean he or she is the person for you. Of course this individual will know more than you—you are new, naïve, and vulnerable on many levels. Because you are at a disadvantage, take your time. Think of joining a religious/spiritual system and tradition like beginning a relationship with a lover. When you first meet someone, things appear wonderful and great, until you spend more time with them and begin to see their true colors, which in some cases are not good. This would be assuming that you've been in a difficult relationship before, and if you have, then you will understand my point. And through experience, hopefully you have learned to choose better relationships and people to be in your life—choosing a religious/spiritual system is no different.

Now that you are familiar with the various types of godparents, you could very well meet someone who could be expert or initiated into all of the above or any combination thereof (but not a woman, because women cannot become babalawos). When looking for a godparent, beware of unscrupulous fakes lurking around to feed on the meek and vulnerable. Beware of those using fictitious names and credentials and those who hide behind websites, forums, and books, waiting for the unknowing to fall prey. Limit your chances of becoming a victim and consider the following:

- Check the credentials and experience of any individual who claims to be a priest. When an individual is initiated into priesthood, there are plenty of witnesses who must attend the ceremony; therefore, you can ask who initiated and trained them, and when and where it occurred. It will be beneficial to find out as much as you can about their religious lineage.

- Investigate their ethics, standards, and expectations for you as an aleyo/godchild.
- Find out if they have a religious support system, whether they are active participants in ritual and ceremony, and if they have constant contact with elders, other iles/houses, and priests and priestesses within the Òrìsà community.

You want someone who:

- Is seasoned and has been around.
- Is positive in mind.
- Knows the rights from the wrongs, and practices accordingly.
- Reinforces independence and free will.
- Is stable and secure in their own personal and spiritual/religious life; their attitude and lifestyle should reflect their priesthood.
- You can bond and build a trusting partnership with.
- Is sensitive to matters of the heart and sexual relations. A godparent is supposed to guide you constructively and spiritually, but does not need to be involved with every aspect of your personal life. Both the godparent/elder in charge and the aleyo/client need to be objective. It is not the responsibility of the godparent/elder to take sides unless there is an obvious issue of a right or wrong. Even then, this could be an awkward position for a godparent to be placed in. In addition, sexual

relations with a godparent are forbidden, and if someone wants sex in exchange for services you should run as fast as you can. In the Lukumi/Yoruba system, this is considered incest unless through divination the Ifa, Òrìsà or spirit speak otherwise. The same holds true for godbrothers and godsisters who are attracted to one another. It is human nature to be physically attracted to or pursue another in your ile. If this is the case, it is recommended that the situation be taken to Ifa, Òrìsà or spirit beforehand to determine what is appropriate, especially for developing relationships. When this is not done or when the relationship is broken, it can prove disastrous for the ile, particularly if the couple shares the same godparent and ile. My recommendation is to set the ground rules ahead of time.

- Is not all drama and no action. Do not become star struck and taken in by dramatic priests and priestesses with bold entrances, fancy talk, charming ways, and grandiose behaviors, or by priests and priestesses who think that only they know what is right and everyone else is wrong. It is not enough for the person to be initiated, give good readings, or have hundreds of godchildren. What should concern you is the *character* that a priest holds on a daily basis. Many priests and priestesses, false or otherwise, sell a good game, and you can become a victim of circumstance. Many times this cannot be helped, because the new jack does not know any better and is, therefore, vulnerable. The only recommendations I can offer at this time are:

    - Get referrals and talk to reputable priests about protocols.
    - Ask questions and do your research.

- If you have access to the Internet, join a couple of reputable Òrìsà groups. For instance, *www.yahoogroups.com* has several where you can read what real priests and priestesses have to offer in terms of valid knowledge.
- As you become familiar with the tradition, set realistic goals and expectations for yourself and for your godparent or ile/house, if possible, especially where finances are concerned.
- Understand that there are no quick fixes and that quick fixes are usually temporary. Long-term effects only occur by getting to the root of the problem. Expect your growth to be a gradual, on-going process. Some will elevate quicker than others for varying reasons; however, everyone has their own time.
- Beware of anyone who wants to send you sacred items through the mail.
- Do not rush into or let anyone else rush you into anything that may make you feel uncomfortable.

Whoever you decide to choose as a godparent, or whatever your choice of ile/house, it should be person or a place that respects confidentiality and trust. This godparent or ile/house should be an asset and not a liability in your life. This is all providing that you, as the godchild/aleyo, listen to the advice given by your ancestors, spirit guides, and/or Òrìsà and that you have chosen a competent godparent or ile. It is imperative that you work diligently on your character and towards making the necessary changes in your own life that will ensure success no matter where you may end up. Ultimate success is up to you and no one else. Build a relationship with your godparent and set realistic expectations for yourself and for your godparent. Understand that your godparent is not God or Òrìsà personified, and know that your godparent will not be able to solve your every problem. However, if your godparent or ile has a problem helping you, then, at a minimum, they should be able to take you to someone of equal or greater experience (such as an elder) who can help you. So do your part to make for an easy relationship/ partnership between you, your godparent, and your ile/house.

Lastly, you want a godparent who is responsible with money. This spiritual/religious system can be very expensive in financial terms. This is a very sensitive subject, especially for people who have lost money for various reasons. I highly recommend that before you turn over any large sums of money to a godparent or elder, first discuss the service to be given, then the price, and then *write it down*. As the client or aleyo, you must learn how to manage your money. Many people fall victim to "financial loss thinking": because of past behaviors, they know that they will spend their money and won't have any available when it's time to get their ceremonies or services done, so they will give over large sums of money well before it's time to receive their services. In the case of giving installments or making down payments, write down the dates and the amounts given. If possible, have a witness or ask for a receipt when cash is given. If an elder feels offended, I'm sorry, but giving money in this spiritual/religious system is no different than any other transaction where receipts are given on a daily basis. This is not about hurting someone's feelings or mistrust; rather, it is all about protection. Actually, a receipt protects both parties, because the reality is people forget over time what was paid. This way there is no confusion.

Once you have chosen a godparent and/or ile to represent and help you, the process toward priesthood will occur in steps. There are two ceremonies that you will undergo that will mark your official entrance into Lukumi/Yoruba. The first ceremony is where you receive *elekes*, the armor of protection from the Òrìsà. Elekes are beaded necklaces with different colors and patterns that belong to each Òrìsà and are usually the formal introduction into the Lukumi/Yoruba tradition within the Afrikan diaspora.

Elekes are sometimes bought in stores or botanicas; however, these beads are not given to a client or godchild without proper consecration. They are not so-called blessed with some words or homemade liquid and just placed around the client or godchild's neck. There is power, prayer, and ritual administered and applied to these necklaces in a ritualistic and ceremonial manner by elders that truly makes these beads sacred. First off, godparents will have dozens of their elekes washed in a *special omiero* (herb water) that is prayed over, sung over, and then fed with animal blood, usually during other ceremonies and initiations that they attend to save time and money. Once the elekes have been empowered, they are usually hung and kept in a clean place, awaiting the arrival of a new client or initiate. Once an individual is ready for this step, they, too, will be cleaned and prayed over. Then they will be presented with the elekes in front of other priests and their godparent's set of Òrìsà to witness and seal the bond of protection that Òrìsà will place around them. The individual is then officially recognized as a member of their ile, and they are then officially under the protection and supervision of their godparent's Òrìsà and the Òrìsà in general.

Each individual who undergoes this ceremony usually receives five standard necklaces that belong to Òrìsà Elegba, Òrìsà Obatala, Òrìsà Oshun, Òrìsà Yemaya, and Òrìsà

Shango. Other Òrìsà necklaces can be received as well, depending on your guardian Òrìsà or if prescribed through divination. Every Òrìsà has its own colors and numbered patterns to specifically represent them and the lineage of that particular ile. For example, Obàtálá is represented with all white beads, except sometimes four red beads are strategically placed throughout the white beads. Yemaya is represented with seven clear beads alternating with seven blue beads. Elegua is represented with one red bead alternating with one black bead, or three red beads alternating with three black beads. Oshun is represented with honey-colored or amber beads in sets of five, with sometimes a red, orange, or yellow bead in between the sets. Shango's necklace is usually one red bead alternating with one white bead.

Not only do elekes represent the Òrìsà, but they are also representative of the ile that you belong to. For instance, the eleke of Shango is red and white, but not all elekes of Shango look alike. This is because godparents will give their clients and godchildren the same pattern of beads that was given to them from their godparent or ile. Some godparents will have a Shango eleke that consists of one white bead alternating with one red bead, while other houses may use six white beads alternating with six red beads—the number six is the number that belongs to Shango. So, depending on the practices of your godparent's ile, this will determine what type of elekes you will receive.

The second ceremony that marks entrance into the Lukumi/ Yoruba religion within the Afrikan diaspora is receiving the *warriors (guerreros)*, which consist of Elegba, Ogun, Ochosi, and Osun. In Afrika, this will vary. According to my knowledge from within the Afrikan diaspora, people have received two sets of warriors. An olorìsà— a male priest/santero—gives one set of warriors, and a babalawo gives the other set. This is important to understand, because the babalawo is a higher priest than an olorìsà, and the warriors that are given are of a different nature, but this does not make one set better than the other. Both have their purposes and are extremely important; however, they are used differently within the religion. One main difference is that if you are given a set of warriors by a babalawo, the only other person who can touch those warriors must be a priest of babalawo status. The Elegba that is given from a babalawo is called eshu (a different energy), and because babalawos are harder to find than priests, you may find yourself stuck when it is time for you to work or feed these warriors. On the other hand, if you receive a set of warriors given by an olorìsà, then you will have a little more flexibility in who you can choose to do work for you.

In some cases, there are individuals who will have both sets, either because it was divined or because they may have been associated with different priests at separate points in their lives. This does not indicate that you should have several different priests working with your warriors, though. You should always try to maintain a relationship with the godparent who you received your warriors from, if at all possible.

Note: A ceremony or initiation is binding. It is a covenant (a sacred agreement or a promise) between you and Olodumare (God), the Òrìsà, the ancestors, and/or spirit guides. In the case of receiving your elekes, you are making a sacred agreement between you, the Òrìsà, and your godparent(s). Many devotees do not understand, nor do the elders emphasize enough, that you are promising the Òrìsà and the ancestors that you will respect and uphold the ethics, the moral obligations, and the secrets of the tradition.

All parties to the covenant are supposed to uphold and observe things that are pleasing to the Òrìsà and the ancestors in order to promote and strengthen a good relationship between them and the divinities, Òrìsà. Because the Afrikans believed that Olodumare, the Òrìsà, and the ancestors are capable of determining and influencing a person's destiny, keeping covenants, keeping your word, and keeping promises to the divinities are extremely important. The Afrikans believed that covenants:

- "Constantly remind humans of their relationship to God.
- Help to establish a union between humans and their fellow man and between humans and their divinities, ancestors, and the Supreme Being.
- Help to ensure mutual trust; thus, covenants have psychological significance and give peace of mind and confidence for people to go about their daily activities.
- Promote good moral behavior. This is due to the fact that people who enter into a covenant relationship try to abide by the terms of the covenant by doing good and refraining from doing or saying anything evil against others. They may fear that they would be punished by the gods or ancestors when they break the terms of the covenant, since the gods or ancestors acted as witnesses to the covenant agreement."[x]
- The negative side of covenants is that many people think that they can make covenants of bribery. They are under the misconception that if they receive ceremonies and initiations it will protect them from their wrongdoings. They also think that they can manipulate the energy of Òrìsà, which would be like trying to contain the wind or put the ocean in a jar. It simply does not work that way; and if you do not

believe it, you can ask all those who are initiated who stole, sold drugs, committed murders, or committed evils against others with witchcraft—they are either sick, are in turmoil, have been hit with misfortune, are in jail, or are dead. The Òrìsà cannot be manipulated or bought, and anyone who thinks so will find themselves in dire circumstances.

Once you have received your elekes and warriors, you now have your foundation. From here it is just a matter of learning as much as you can from your godparents and your ile. Between the point that you have received your elekes and warriors up until the point of priesthood, the day that you receive kari-ocha, you will receive many divinations/readings with messages from your ancestors, Òrìsà, or Ifa, if you are seeing a babalawo. And during the process of receiving divinations/readings, one of the more important ones will be the reading that *"marks your head"*. This process in Santeria/Lukumi is called *bajado*; a divination ritual done by an oriate to determine a client's guardian Òrìsà. This process is so delicate and important that I would like to share some words of wisdom from a very well-known elder within the Òrìsà community, the late Baba Alfred Davis, ibae, about the "marking of one's head."

Baba Alfred's words:

Subj: Thanks & Questions--Further comments!
Date: 98-07-01 12:00:46 EDT From: ADavis9727
To: Orishalist
Ago OrishaList!

l. Many times the errors are on the part of the uninitiated. Example: many want to know, and many insist, at the time of their very first 'reading', upon asking and knowing which is the Orisha of their head. Many want to know this very early, even before they begin their practice of Orisha worship.

They 'allegedly' want to establish a devotion to a particular Orisha. If the baba/iyalosha is not highly skilled in dillogun divination in determining the Orisha, errors can be made at the start. Even if a person is read first by a babalawo, who uses the opele to determine the Orisha of the person in one reading, there are the possibilities of errors being made. There are 'correct' processes for 'marking' Orishas for heads and if this is not followed, then errors and problems result. The best approach for a neophyte or aleyo to follow is to begin on the path to the Orishas by ACCEPTING AND LOVING ALL OF THE ORISHAS...and later on, be ready to be 'claimed' by them, or have your head correctly 'marked.' Many make errors as they want to pick and choose their favorite Orisha, and want that specific Orisha because of the qualities that they admire in their 'chosen' Orisha. Every young man studying to become a drummer wants to be initiated as Omo-Shango! ...when in reality, many are Omo-Oshuns and Omo-Yemojas. Many of the macho types have a problem accepting a female Orisha as their head Orisha. Many young women prefer only Oshun as they admire and want her 'beauty' and ultra-femininity!

An Aleyo should not 'settle' with the idea of devotion to a particular Orisha, until the correct one has been verified! Determining the correct Orisha can be very difficult and one should not be in a rush for that information during their first 'reading' or at the onstart of their path to Orisha! The aleyo who insists upon being initiated to their 'chosen' Orisha, rather than accept the one 'marked' by Ifa or claimed directly by an Orisha, is making a grave mistake. The godparent that 'knowingly' goes ahead and crowns the wrong Orisha adds to and compounds the grave mistake.

The weight of the mistake can fall on the innocent 'aleyo' as no initiation can take place without MONEY! Money is the final 'go-ahead' on the initiation plans. It's the bottom line. If the aleyo knows that the godparent is planning to initiate the wrong Orisha, then it's a simple matter for the aleyo to withhold all funds, until all cloudy issues (which Orisha is the correct one?) are cleared and settled amicably, and all parties are in agreement.

2. Even in a bembe, when one is face to face with an Orisha, the Orisha can claim a person. Even in that instance, if the person is an 'aleyo' the matter should be verified by Ifa. Orishas, through 'possessions' can also see the quality of Ori and 'Iwa' that a person has, and claim that person as their child. This happened to me, even after initiation. It matters not...as I love them all and work diligently with all. There were never any repercussions! So, why should I be concerned? I felt blessed, gratified, and up-lifted that another Orisha wanted me, even after initiation.

3. Maria used the term 'beaten' by the Orisha. Others use the term 'punished' by the Orisha. I think that the term punished or punishment is a 'Christian' hang-over, like the belief in the 'concept' of punishment for sins. I don't believe in either.

4. I think that what has been left out by all of the writers are the consciences of all parties concerned. After making these grave errors, the negativities and guilts begin to 'eat' at the consciences of all parties involved. To me, their consciences 'beat' them, not the Orishas. To me, that is their living "hell" in what (an error) produces in later experiences and the horrible consequences in their lives. It may have very little or nothing to do directly with the will or actions of the Orishas. Of course, this is my opinion! We obey the Orishas, but we still have free-will! People have a tendency to blame everything in the universe for what happens to them and for their misfortunes...they blame everything external to themselves. They blame Esu, iku, negative spirits, ar'-aiye, their neighbors, their in-laws or criminal out-laws... everything and everyone but themselves, for their poor, improper choices and incorrect actions! Remember, in life--for every action, there is a re-action! That's one of the fundamental spiritual laws of the Universe-- deity or no deity! Know what to expect as a consequence to your thoughts, words or actions! Be willing to accept the consequences!

Blessings of the Orishas to all!
Odabo - Alfred Davis- OmiToki

The marking of your head can be so controversial that it would benefit you to really take your time to ensure the correct processes are done. Do not be in a rush; this is unnecessary unless you are in a state of crisis. In the years prior to receiving ocha, I placed myself in unnecessary situations because I always felt that I needed to hurry to get things done. The tricky part was that the services prescribed to me were services that I needed, but the people were not doing them correctly; being new, I didn't know any better. I thought I was being efficient and on top of things by getting them done quickly. I realized later in my life that I did not need to move as quickly as I did, and had I just stepped back and waited a little bit, I would have noticed some uncool things going on. Many times you will have things done correctly, but you must be leery of the many unskilled priests or priestesses who can make things far worse than what they are, all because they do not possess the knowledge. My recommendation is to tread lightly and have patience—it could save your life.

As you continue to receive divinations/readings, many things will be revealed. The divination process will determine what is good for you and what is taboo (forbidden), and what things you can and cannot do (restrictions); you will receive warnings of what things to heed; and you will be advised emotionally, mentally, and financially on how to proceed with your life from that point forward. The godchild or the client needs to understand that taboos and restrictions are not to cause hurt; they are the way that the ancestors and Òrìsà offer protection from bad circumstances. For instance, I was told not to eat seedy or grainy fruits like pears, because the seeds or grains could get caught in my throat and I could choke to death. It is up to me to either listen or risk the circumstances. The whole concept of taboos and prohibitions comes from our Afrikan ancestors. Taboos are meant to keep you spiritually strong and protected. They believed that taboos were important because they prevented certain calamities in society. For instance, the Afrikans had a taboo that forbade sexual intercourse in the bush in order to prevent people from being bitten by poisonous creatures like snakes, spiders, and scorpions. Listen and heed the warnings of your divination sessions, because disobeying can put you in an unwanted situation; it is also considered disrespectful and an offense to the supreme being, the ancestors, and your spirit guides.

Until you become a priest or priestess, try to remain as active as you can in your spiritual ile, while at the same time doing whatever it is you need to do to ensure success in your life. Take care of your ancestors and your spirit guides as much as possible before your initiation. Some godparents and iles will organize a mass/misa/séance to identify your ancestors and spirit guides/eguns to give proper acknowledgement and respect to those spirits. But remember, some godparents and iles do not work with spiritualism (mass/misa/séance) on this level. They simply feel that the spirit guides/eguns will have an interest in you whether you acknowledge them or not. There is nothing wrong with this, because this is what works for them.

In many Afrikan cultures, people believe that human suffering—such as illness, accidents, poverty, and misfortune—can be attributed to angry, unsettled ancestors who have not been properly venerated, who may not have had proper burials, or who have simply been forgotten; therefore, all that can be done to appease the ancestors is also done to encourage ease in life. Many believe that frequent rituals and ancestor reverence can also affect the most fundamental characteristics or karma of family members so that each generation and future generations will change for the better, eventually fading away old problems or making so-called curses become more manageable.

In conclusion to all that has been said in this book, I will reiterate that you should do your research and understand as much as you can about the past and present of both Lukumi and Yoruba. Learn all that you can about your own history or lineage and the accomplishments and failures of your ancestors. This may give you some insight about which direction you need to go. To understand the culture of Lukumi/ Yoruba, you should understand what our ancestors once understood in their day of practice. It is so important to hold onto your heritage and to keep the names of your ancestors alive so that we can continue to live individually, as a community, and eventually as a society.

Failing to preserve your heritage or heal your ancestral line could eventually mark the Black and Hispanic races to extinction, because our own problems will consume us and we will be wiped off the face of the earth. Extinction does not necessarily mean that we will be dead physically, but we may be dead politically, economically, and socially. We need our ancestors to commune with us to help us strategically survive this world. Things are getting worse because we are hurting ourselves mentally, physically, and emotionally. We are not taking care of our minds, bodies, and souls, and this is what we need the Òrìsà and the ancestors to teach us. We need their energies to help strengthen us individually and as a community. We need communal and societal solidarity, as our ancestors once ensured, and I hope that anyone following this path of reverence understands that Òrìsà and the ancestors tell us things both negatively and positively only to help us.

Without experience, it will be hard to determine what is right for you and what is not. No one can say at this moment where you will end up and with what ceremonies, correct or not. The only thing you can do is pray to your ancestors, higher spirits, guardian angels, or guardian Òrìsà to put you in the right place at the right time. And in the interim, if you just so happen to encounter a bad experience, despite your prayers, then understand that even the bad experiences are needed in your evolutionary process. Many in this religion, both old and young, encounter experiences both good and bad, but this is a part of the process. Lord knows I have had my share of experiences, but in all reality, if I had not had them I would not be able to write this for you now.

When you are naïve, unsure, and vulnerable because you do not know what is right, turn to your ancestors and guardian spirits for guidance, and trust that they will lead you to the place where you need to be at that time. You may go through several people and iles and through some rough times before you end up in the right place, but know that it is not a waste; this, too, is part of the process. No matter what choices we make and no matter who is chosen to guide us, nothing is wasted as long as we learn from it.

I wish you the best, and may God and the good spirits bless you with health, prosperity, and success. Àse!

GLOSSARY

Aganju – Aganju is the *Òrìsà* of volcanos. Aganju is an Òrìsà of the ancients. Aganju is a force that is essential for growth, as well as a cultivator of civilizations. Like the volcano, Aganju structures the foundation upon which societies are built and is the vehicle for the production of vast amounts of wealth and commerce needed for complex development. Aganju has the role in assisting humans in overcoming great physical and psychological barriers. Aganju is noted for his renowned strength and his ability to bring about radical change *(see Wikipedia, Free Encyclopedia Online)*.

aleyo – is *Lukumi* terminology to mean an individual who is considered an outsider to an Òrìsà-based community because he/she has not been initiated into priesthood, but aspires to practice the traditions of Lukumi/Yoruba.

Allan Kardec – known world-wide as the Codifier of the *Spiritist Doctrine*. Kardec was born as Hippolyte Leon Denizard Rivail in Lyon, France - the 3rd of October 1804.

ancestor spirits – deceased family members of the same blood.

Àṣe – a yoruban word that means *"power"* or *"command"*. One who has Àṣe has the power to make things happen; i.e., one can have Àṣe of the tongue or Àṣe of luck, etc.

babalawo – means *"father of secrets"*. A male priest who has been initiated into the mysteries of Ifa/Yoruba.

bajado –a divination done to determine a client's guardian Òrìsà. This particular divination is usually done by an Oba/Oriate or Babalawo.

bakulu – are the ancestors, most specific to the Congolese.

bembe – a drumming celebration to the Òrìsà. The drums are played in a specific pattern or rhythm accompanied by dance and praise songs to call forth the Òrìsà to earth. The Òrìsà are instigated to join in on the celebration bringing with them messages that can uplift all who attend the celebration.

botanica – a spiritual/religious store that sells products such as anointing oils, books, candles, herbs, powders, rare and sacred items or products to those who are practicing some sort of spiritual-based system such as Palo, Santeria, Vodou, Wicca, etc.

boveda – a spanish word for "altar". This altar is used for communicating with ones ancestors and spirit guides.

Candomblé - is an Afrikan-originated or Afro-Brazilian religion, practiced chiefly in Brazil.

cascarilla – white eggshell powder usually used in spiritual baths or Santeria spells and rituals.

Congo/Kongo - The Bakongo or the Kongo people (meaning "hunter"), most often referred to as Congolese, live along the Atlantic coast of Africa. Kongo is also a word to describe a type of spirit guide.

dillogun – nickname for its full name, *merindinlogun*,

which is the practice of casting 16 cowrie shells used by initiated priests or priestesses within the Lukumi, Santeria, Yoruban tradition.

divination – a kind of road map to one's life path and even their destiny. It is the practice used to reveal accurate, hidden information or truth about the past, present, and future by a person with spiritual gifts, or what are believed to be supernatural means.

diviner – a person that interprets messages from various realms of the spirit world. They use their own type of oracle, source, or tool to help them reveal the mysteries of life.

ebbo/ebo – *"life force offering"*. This offering/sacrifice is usually prescribed to either give thanks to God, the Òrìsà, the ancestors, and/ or your guides for all your blessings or to block the progression of negative conditions and circumstances.

egun – generic word for spirit guides inclusive of one's ancestors.

egungun – ancestors, only those considered kin (*family of the same blood*). Egungun is a secret society of Yoruba people who believe in the continued existence of ancestors in the lives of the living.

Elegba – an Òrìsà known as "the messenger" and "owner of the crossroads."

eleke/elekes - beaded necklaces with different colors and patterns that belong to each Òrìsà and are usually the formal introduction into the Lukumi, Santeria, Yoruban tradition within the Afrikan Diaspora.

epo – palm oil.

espiritista – a spiritual medium and/or psychic that interprets messages from the spirit world.

Esu – an *Òrìsà* deity known as the divine messenger of the West Afrikan religious tradition called *Ifa*.

Ewe – a people located on the southeast corner of Ghana.

foribale – a method of salutation to an *Òrìsà* or elder priest/priestess within the religion of Lukumi, Santeria, Yoruba. The salutation will depend on whether the guardian Òrìsà is male or female.

Gelede – "one of the spiritual "feminine" systems of the Yoruban people who believe women, mostly elderly woman, possess certain extraordinary power equal to or greater than that of the gods and ancestors, a view that is reflected in praises acknowledging them as "our mothers", "the gods of society", and "owners of the world". With this power, the "mothers" can be either beneficent or destructive. They can bring health, wealth, and fertility to the land and its people, or they can bring disaster – epidemic, drought, pestilence." *(see bibliography - Gelede).*

guerreros – spanish word that means *"warriors"*. The warriors consist of Elegba, Ogun, Ochosi, Osun. These Òrìsàs are received together in one initiation/ceremony.

gypsy spirit – a spirit guide that has similar characteristics to that of a fortune teller.

hitana – spanish word for "gypsy". See *gypsy spirit.*

hoodoo - a form of predominantly Afrikan-American

traditional folk magic. It is a tradition of magical practice that developed from the melding of various cultures and magical traditions. Hoodoo incorporates practices from Afrikan and Native American traditions, as well as some European magical practices and grimoires.

hudu – *Original Ewe spelling. See hoodoo for definition.*

ibae – a *lukumi* phrase that means "I pay homage [to the dead]."

Ifa – although there isn't a literal translation; Ifa is a cosmology that refers to a religious/spiritual tradition, ethical understanding, a process of spiritual transformation and a *set of scriptures* that are the basis for a very complex system of divination. Therefore, Ifa is the embodiment of knowledge and wisdom and the highest form of divination practice among the Lukumi, Santeria, and Yoruban people.

Ile – a (house/place of individuals that venerate *Òrìsà*, ancestors and *egun*). The Ile has an elder or group of elders that provide teachings and guidance on a formal or informal basis.

indio – Spanish word for American Indian/Native American spirit guide.

juju – is an aura or other magical property, usually having to do with spirits or luck, which is bound to a specific object; it is also a term for the object. Juju also refers to the spirits and ghosts in West Afrikan lore as a general name.

kari-ocha – an *Òrìsà* initiation/ceremony; considered to be a marriage between the initiate and their guardian *Òrìsà* (this guardian Òrìsà or divinity is the one that was assigned to govern over this person at birth).

libation - a ritual pouring of a drink as an offering to a god/goddess or the ancestors. In most Afrikan cultures, the libation ritual of pouring a drink or water to the "Gods and to the ancestors" is an essential religious and ceremonial tradition.

lucumi/lukumi – translation to mean *"my friend"* in the Afrikan Diaspora.

Macumba - a word of Afrikan (Bantu) origins.

Madama – known as "la madama"; a very hard working spirit called upon to remove evils, bad luck, and to bring good fortune.

maferefun – a term meaning *"praise be"* or *"all power be to"*.

mass – different from that given in "church". Also called séance, performed to commune and honor the ancestors and spirits of the dead. This gathering typically includes altar setup, prayers, singing, offerings, and the possession of mediums (known as "trance mediumship") by spirits.

medicine wheel – also called sacred hoops, stones laid into a particular pattern on the ground by the indigenous, representing the journey each person must take to find their own path through ancient teachings, astronomy, healings, and rituals.

medium (mediumship) - a main form of practice in spiritualism where individuals have the "spiritual ability or gift" to communicate with those in the realm of spirit. Most indigenous and Afrikan diasporic traditions include mediumship as a central focus of their spiritual practices.

merindinlogun – see *dillogun*.

misa – see *mass*.

negro – a Spanish word to describe a spirit of Afrikan descent or of a darkened skin color.

nfumbe – Palo spirits of the dead. See *palo*.

nganga – a Bantu term for herbalist or spiritual healer in many societies of the Afrikan diaspora such as those in Haiti, Brazil and Cuba. Also refers to a tripod iron cauldron filled with various ingredients, specific to the religion of Palo; representing the ritual nucleus and focus of power. The ngangas are consecrated with particular prayers, songs, sticks, bones, dirt, and herbs that are sacred to a particular spirit (nfumbe) of Palo and are only given to individuals who have gone through all the proper ceremonies.

Obatala – is an Òrìsà and through the power of God, the Supreme Being, made human bodies, and Olorun (God) breathed life into them. Obatala is also *the owner of all heads*. Obatala (King of the white cloth), must never be worshipped with palm wine, palm oil or salt.

obi – represents the coconut itself; but also used as a system of divination (4 pieces of coconut) amongst the Lukumi/Yoruban people.

obi abata – sacred kolanut which has four separable segments— two males and two females, representing the primary masculine and feminine forces of the universe.

ocha – see *kari ocha*.

Ochosi - (also spelt, Ososi, Oxosi, Osawsi), is an *Òrìsà* of the forest. Ochosi is a hunter and patron of justice. We call upon Ochosi when we need direction for he never misses his mark.

Ogun - the traditional warrior and seen as a powerful *Òrìsà* of metal work, particularly iron. In Haitian Vodou and Yoruba theology, Ogun (or Ogoun, Ogum, Ogou) is a loa and *Òrìsà*, who presides over fire, iron, hunting, politics and war. He is the patron of the blacksmiths and is usually displayed with his attributes: machete or sabre, rum and tobacco *(see Wikipedia, Free Encyclopedia Online)*.

Olodumare – supreme being "God". Also called by various names in the Yoruba language such as Eledumare, Olofin-Orun, Eleda, and Olorun.

Olokun - Olokun is an *Òrìsà* experienced in male and female personifications, depending on what region of West Africa. Olokun is personified in several human characteristics; patience, endurance, sternness, observation, meditation, appreciation for history, future visions, and royalty. Olokun also signifies profound wisdom, material wealth, psychic abilities, dreaming, fertility, meditation, mental health and water-based healing *(see Wikipedia, Free Encyclopedia Online)*.

Olorun - also referred to as Olodumare as well as Eledumare, and Eleda among other names, is a word for God (the Supreme Being), in the Yoruba language.

omiero – an herbal water that is hand prepared with fresh green herbs and plants, specifically prepared to bring blessings, to remove negativity, and to uplift the spiritual and physical body of the person being helped. Mainly used by initiates of Lukumi/Yoruba faith in giving birth to sacred items of the Òrìsà in special ceremonies.

opa iku - is a summoning stick used to call the ancestors and/or spirits to your aid.

opele – sacred chain used for divining by a *Babalawo*.

opon ifa – divination tray used by a *Babalawo*.

Òrìsà – (also spelled Orisha or Orixa) are manifestations of Olodumare (God) in the Afrikan Diaspora and Yoruban spiritual/religious system. Òrìsà are the Afrikan gods/goddesses that rule the natural forces within the universe, i.e., the ocean waters are ruled by Yemaya/Olokun, the wind is ruled by Oya, and volcanic activity is ruled by Aganju. This religion has found its way throughout the world and is practiced throughout areas of Nigeria, the Republic of Benin, Togo, Brazil, Cuba, Dominican Republic, Guyana, Jamaica, Puerto Rico, Suriname, Trinidad and Tobago, the United States, the West Indies and Venezuela among others *(see Wikipedia, Free Encyclopedia Online)*.

Orunmila – *Òrìsà* of destiny and prophecy. He is recognized as second only to Olodumare (God) and "eleri ipin" (witness to creation). Orunmila is also known as Orula & Orunla. Orunmila is regarded as a wise man or sage.

Oshun - Goddess *(Òrìsà)* who reigns over love, intimacy, beauty, wealth and diplomacy. Oshun is the "unseen mother present at every gathering", because Oshun is the Yoruba understanding of the cosmological forces of water, moisture, and attraction. Therefore she is omnipresent and omnipotent. In Yoruban scripture, we are reminded that "no one is an enemy to water" and therefore everyone has need of and should respect and revere Oshun *(see Wikipedia, Free Encyclopedia Online).*

Oya - An *Òrìsà* warrior-goddess of wind, lightning, fertility, fire and magic. She creates hurricanes and tornadoes and guards the underworld. She is called Oya-Yansan, which means "mother of nine." The faithful often salute her by saying *"Hekua hey Yansa".* Oya manifests in Creation in the forms as sudden and drastic change, strong storms, and the flash of the marketplace *(see Wikipedia, Free Encyclopedia Online).*

palera/palero – practitioner of the spiritual system of *Palo.*

Palo – means "stick". Palo is also a word used to describe a type of spiritual system derived from the Congolese people in Africa. See *"palo mayombe".*

palo mayombe – one of the main sects of *Palo,* spiritual system that centers around the successful use of amulets/charms, firmas, herbs, incantations, or any kind of strong medicine in order to take action and influence, alter or intervene in unfavorable developments.

potencia – house of *Palo.*

prendas – see *nganga.*

reader – see *diviner.*

ritual - a ritual is a set of actions, often thought to have symbolic value, the performance of which is usually prescribed by a religion or by the traditions of a community by religious or political laws because of the perceived efficacy of those actions.

rootwork – see *hoodoo*.

Sambi – correctly spelled Nzami, high God, of the Congolese people in Africa. The God praised in the religion/spiritual systems of *Palo*.

Santeria – Term for *Òrìsà* worship as it developed in Cuba; the English translation from the Spanish word is "worship of the saints". Afro-Caribbean religious tradition derived from traditional beliefs of the Yoruba people of Nigeria. The Santería/Yoruba tradition comprises a hierarchical structure according to priesthood level and authority. Òrìsà "ile" or temples are usually governed by Òrìsà priests or Babalorìsàs, "fathers of Òrìsà", or Iyalorìsàs, "mothers of Òrìsà" *(see Wikipedia, Free Encyclopedia Online)*.

Sango – One of the most popular Òrìsà; God of Thunder & Lightning. Sango was a royal ancestor of the Yoruba as he was the third king of the Oyo Kingdom. The energy given from this Deity of Thunder is also a major symbol of Afrikan resistance against an enslaving European culture. He rules the color red and white; his sacred number is 6; his symbol is the oshe (double-headed axe), which represents swift and balanced justice. He is owner of the Bata (3 double-headed drums) and of music in general, as well as the Art of Dance and Entertainment *(see Wikipedia, Free Encyclopedia Online)*.

Spiritist – a follower of the *Spiritist Doctrine*.

Spiritism – a doctrine that has its foundation in the relationship between the material world and spirit, i.e., the beings of the invisible world.

Spiritist Doctrine – the philosophy that deals with the

nature, the origin, and the destiny of spirits, as well as their relationship with the material/physical world.

spirits – deceased beings of the invisible world. They populate the entire universe and can be found beyond the boundaries of the physical world.

spiritualism - a scientific, philosophical, and religious practice that proves the continuity of life after death through demonstrated communication between mediums/ spiritualists and those who reside in the spirit world.

tierra – territory.

trunk/tronko – a lineage.

Vodou/Vodoun – correct spelling of voodoo. Vodou is a legitimate religious system that derived from the traditions of the Afrikan slaves and upholds customary structures, levels of hierarchy, ethics, restrictions, and taboos; ceremonial initiations are mandatory.

vovoda – see *boveda*.

Yemaya – is an *Òrìsà*, originally of the Yoruba religion, who has become prominent in many Afro-American religion. She is the essence of motherhood, and a protector of children. She is the Queen of the Ocean, the patron deity of the fishermen and the survivors of shipwrecks, the feminine principle of creation and the spirit of moonlight. Her name is a contraction of Yoruba words: *"Yeye emo eja"* that mean "Mother whose children are like fishes *(see Wikipedia, Free Encyclopedia Online)*.

Yoruba – The Yoruba religion is the religious beliefs and practices of the Yoruba people both in Africa and in the

New World, where it has influenced or given birth to several Afro-American religions such as Santería in Cuba and Umbanda and Candomblé in Brazil. Though specific numbers are unknown, it is possibly the largest Afrikan born religion in the world.

BIBLIOGRAPHY

The following books and websites have truly inspired my thoughts and my writing and may prove helpful to you as well.

Buckland, Raymond. *Gypsy Witchcraft & Magic*. St. Paul, MN: Llewellyn Publications, 1998.

Conde, Maryse. *I, Tituba, Black Witch of Salem*. New York: Ballantine Books, 1994.

Cunningham, Scott. *Cunningham's Encyclopedia of Magical Herbs*. St. Paul, MN: Llewellyn Publications, 2000.

Dey, Charmaine. *The Magic Candle: Facts and Fundamentals of Ritual Candle-Burning*. Plainview, NY: Original Publications, 1982.

Dreller, Larry. *Beginner's Guide to Mediumship*. York Beach, ME: Samuel Weiser, Inc., 1997.

Drewal, Henry John and Drewal, Margaret Thompson. *Gelede – Art and Female Power among the Yoruba*. Bloomington, ID. Indiana University Press 1990

Fama, Chief. *Fundamentals of Yoruba Religion (Orisa Worship)*. San Bernardino, CA: Ile Orunmila Communications, 1993.

Fatunmbi, Awo Fa'lokun. Ogun – *Ifa and The Spirit of Iron.* Bronx, NY. Original Publications, 1992

Fatunmbi, Awo Fa'lokun. Esu-Elegba – *Ifa and The Divine Messenger.* Bronx, NY. Original Publications, 1992

Fatunmbi, Awo Fa'lokun. Shango – *Ifa and The Spirit of Lightning.* Bronx, NY. Original Publications, 1992

Fatunmbi, Awo Fa'lokun. Yemoja/Olokun – *Ifa and The Spirit of the Ocean.* Bronx, NY. Original Publications, 1992

Furlong, David. *"Clearing Ancestral Blocks." Ancestral Healing.* Website: http://www.kch42.dial pipex.com/ancestral.htm, 1994.

Holmes, Ernest. *"The Science of Mind."* New York, NY. United Church of Religious Science, 1926, 1938. Penguin Group, 2010

Houngan Hector. *Real Voodoo.* Website: http://www.ezilikonnen.com, 2008

Hunter-Hindrew MEd, Vivian. Mami Wata Vodoun Amengansie Chief Priestess, (aka Mama Zogbe). *"Vodoun ('Voodoo'): The Religious Practices of Southern Slaves in America, a History of Religious Persecution and Suppression."* Website: http://www.mamiwata.com/ history.html, 2005.

Janssen, Division of Ortho-McNeil-Janssen Pharmaceuticals, Inc. *"Schizophrenia."* MentalWellness.com. Website: http://www.mental-wellness.com/mentalwellness/sch_schizophrenia.html, 2004.

Karade, Baba Ifa. *The Handbook of Yoruba Religious Concepts.* York Beach, ME: Samuel Weiser, Inc., 1994.

Kardec, Allan. *The Book on Mediums: Guide for Mediums and Invocators.* York Beach, ME: Samuel Weiser, Inc., 1989.

Kardec, Allan. *Collection of Selected Prayers.* Bronx, NY: De Pablo International Inc., North American Import & Services Co., 1989.

Kardec, Allan. *Introduction to the Spiritist Philosophy.* Philadelphia, PA, Allan Kardec Educational Society, 2004

Lele, Ocha'Ni. *The Dilloggun-The Orishas, Proverbs, Sacrifices, and Prohibitions of Cuban Santeria.* Rochester, Vermont. Destiny Books. 2003

Malbrough, Ray T. *The Magical Power of the Saints*: Evocations & Candle Rituals. St. Paul, MN: Llewelyn Publications, 2002.

Mettle-Nunoo, E. A. and B. A. Hons, Legon. *"Ahithophel's Series, West African Traditional Religion."* 1993.

Mickaharic, Draja. *Spiritual Cleansings – A Handbook of Psychic Self- Protection.* Boston, MA. Red Wheel/Weiser, Inc. 1982, 2003.

Owomoyela, Oyekan. *Yoruba Proverbs.* Lincoln, NE. University of Nebraska Press., 2005

Palmer, Lynne. *Money Magic.* Las Vegas, NV: Star Bright Publishers, 1996.

Palokongo, Cabildo. *Kanda7Tumba.* http://www.kanda7tumba.net

Riva, Anna. *Candle Burning Magic: A Spellbook of Rituals for Good and Evil.* Toluca Lake, CA: International Imports, 1980.

Schulman, Martin. *Karmic Astrology: The Moon's Nodes*

and Reincarnation. York Beach, ME: Samuel Weiser, Inc., 1975.

The New Webster's Comprehensive Dictionary Deluxe Edition. American International Press, 1989.

Wales, Jimmy and Sanger, Larry. *Wikipedia, The Free Encyclopedia Online.* Wikimedia Foundation. Launched 2001. Website: http:// en.wikipedia.org/wiki/Wikipedia

ADDITIONAL SUGGESTED RESOURCES

The intent of the **National African Religious Congress** (NARC) is to bring unity to all religious cultures. As a unifying organization, NARC's Board of Directors consists of Priests, Priestesses, Babalawos, Iyalorisas, and Nanas from Ghana, Nigeria, Brazil, Cuba, South Africa, England, Trinidad & Tobago, Puerto Rico, and numerous states across America. Link: www.narcworld.com, 2006.

The **Lukumi Church of Orisa** is a not-for-profit organization dedicated to the preservation and devotion of all Afro-Cuban cultures and the mother cultures from which they sprung. The Lukumi Church is a cultural as well as spiritual institution that wishes to bring the richness of the Diaspora to a wider audience. Link: www.lukumichurch.org.

Perry, James. *"African Roots of African-American Culture."* The Black Collegian Online. Link: www.black-collegian.com/issues/1998-12/ africanroots12.shtml, 2005.

FOOTNOTES

1. While reading this book, you may wonder why I spell Amerikan and Afrikan with the letter "k" instead of the letter "c". My purpose is to recapture the "k" from the Afrikan language, which was stripped away from our Afrikan ancestors. I want to bring special attention to these words and to emphasize the need to reconnect with the roots of our Afrikan language and worship that are our birthright. I am rebelling against the European and Western methodologies that were forced on our Afrikan predecessors, so I have decided to get rid of the "c" and place "k" in its original and proper place—giving our Afrikan ancestors a traditional identity in my book.

2. *National Spiritualist Association of Churches*. Lily Dale, NY, 2012. www.nsac.org

3. *Unknown*

4. Referenced from *"Hoodoo - In Theory and Practice - An Introduction to African-American Rootwork"* by Catherine Yronwode, copyright 1995-2003. Lucky Mojo Curio Co., online article at http://luckymojo.com/hoodoo.html

5. Referenced from *"Hoodoo - In Theory and Practice - An Introduction to African-American Rootwork"* by Catherine Yronwode, copyright 1995-2003. Lucky Mojo Curio Co., online article at http://luckymojo.com/hoodoo.html

6. Hunter-Hindrew MEd, Vivian. Mami Wata Vodoun Amengansie Chief Priestess, (aka Mama Zogbe). *"Vodoun ('Voodoo'): The Religious Practices of Southern Slaves in America, a History of Religious Persecution and Suppression."* Website: http://www.mamiwata.com/ history.html, 2005.

7. Contributed by Palo Kongo, Cabildo

8. The entire sections on *Haitian Vodou, Sanse, and Dominican Vodou (pp. 214-218)* were written with permission and contributed by Houngan Hector - website: http://www.ezilikonnen.com

9. Karade, Baba Ifa. *The Handbook of Yoruba Religious Concepts (p. 47), 1994.* Referenced from Muhammed Ali, The Muslim Prayer Book (Ahmaduiyya, 1938) pp. 11-14.

10. Xavier, Franciso Candido. *In the Domain of Mediumship by the Spirit of Andre Luiz (p. 100),* 2006

x. Mettle-Nunoo, E.A. and B.A. Hons, Legon. *"Ahithophel's Series"*

xi. *Aho Mitakuye Oyasin* is a traditional Lakota Sioux prayer, with its opening phrase used as a refrain in many Lakota prayers and songs. *(see Wikipedia, Free Encyclopedia Online).*

xii. *Love Matters*, Xavier, Franciso Candido. Fonte Viva. By the Spirit Emmanuel. 23. Ed. Rio de Janeiro. Feb. 1999. Item 91, p. 211-212.

ABOUT THE AUTHOR
"For it is from the darkness that we find all the answers."

Aladokun is known as a wonderful spiritual teacher and advisor, guiding many to a better position in life. In addition, she is committed to and knows that healing is required on all levels: spirit, mind, and body. And because people gravitate toward different healing modalities, Aladokun has expanded her spiritual scope to include bodywork; giving people other ways to bring spiritual balance and wellness into their lives.

As a Certified Massage and Sound Therapist, Aladokun is able to use her intuitive abilities, the Àṣe of Obatala (power, light and healing) upon those who suffer physically, emotionally, mentally and energetically. She says, "Today, people are under great stress and they need all the help that they can get. If I can give someone relief through massage and/or sound therapy vs. ritual then I'm still doing what I was born to do."

She is dedicated to her spiritual studies and has a compassionate commitment to knowledge and understanding of her culture. She continues to share her vision; promoting the education of mind, body, and spirit through the inspiration of articles, poetry, prayer, rituals, veneration, health, and healing.

Oba Ilari Aladokun was born and raised in New York City and has lived in New Jersey for the past several years. She is a priestess of Yoruba/Lukumi and has practiced spiritualism for over a decade. She has been initiated into several mysteries, including receiving the Hand of Ifa (Mano de Orula) in January 2000 and Palo Mayombe in July 2000. Shortly thereafter, she reached the seat of Kariocha and was initiated in August 2000 in Havana, Cuba, crowned Obatala. She holds several healing certificates: Usui Reiki Master Teacher, Registered Lightarian Reiki Master Facilitator, a Certified Intuitive Counselor of the National Spiritualist Association, and Ordained as a Spiritualist Minister.

Aladokun is available for private consultations, workshops and presentations. The author may be emailed at: ancestorpaths@aol.com.

253

SACRED ME PENDANTS
BY ALADOKUN

"Sacred Me Pendants" were created to honor our connection to Mother Earth as one of our greatest benefactors. Each "Sacred Me Pendant" illustrates the abundance, protection, and beauty that the Earth Mother offers us each and everyday. Earth supports us and reminds us that there is plenty to acquire and plenty to go around; however, you must remember that receiving abundance is a matter of knowing it is yours to claim.

These pendants are unique and original designs handmade by me with lots of love, prayer, and care. Made with the Àṣe of Òrìṣànlá; high vibrational and made with natural materials of the highest quality. As a beacon of light, not only can you wear your pendant for any occasion but you can use your pendant to enhance or add positive energy to your meditation, prayer, and/or manifestation work.

Visit Shop:
http://www.etsy.com/shop/SacredMePendants

With Love, Aladokun

SACRED STONE MASSAGE

The ancient spiritual system of Yoruba/Ifa and my ancestors inspired the creation of Sacred Stone Massage™. While massaging a client one day, a strong vision appeared to me revealing the healing powers of the Sacred Stones. As a priestess of Òrìṣànlá, the Deity of Purity & Light, I've come to know that everything in nature has a soul even something as dense as a stone. And in order to access the primordial life force energies that live within, special stones were chosen to go through days of ancestral prayers and ceremony. Therefore, the stones used in the Sacred Stone Massage™ have been consecrated (blessed & prayed over) by authentic (Afrikan) Ifa priests and priestesses who work hand in hand with the forces of nature. These Elders have a long and extensive lineage of divination, indigenous medicine, spiritual power and healing. This form of practice is a way of life, the traditional way of living in harmony with all things. Humbleness, patience, and self improvement are core values taught to me by my Elders and these are the virtues that exemplify the power of the Sacred Stones.

The Sacred Stone Massage is for those seeking awareness and a spiritual journey of emotional, physical, mental, and/or soul healing. For this reason, the hot stones used in this special massage are unique in that they have been activated, ceremonially, to fully benefit your healing process. These stones are grounding and powerful protectors. Your treatment is a direct connection to ancestral forces that are powerful allies in spiritual growth and healing. This can help you to initiate your inner journey and connect inwardly to a higher "Source" of power. Such practice is appropriate for anyone who, for whatever reason, calls upon Spirit for intervention in their lives, making this type of treatment sacred and intuitive.

FOR ADDITIONAL INFORMATION – VISIT WEBSITE:
www.apsdynamicmassage.com

ISORO ORUN
ORIKI ORISAS
(Volume One)
English Translation
$20.00

www.abalayenifa.org
http://www.blogtalkradio.com/oluwo
Email: info@abalayenifa.org

RATE THIS BOOK

Write a Review – Your opinion on the information given in this book is greatly appreciated. Rate this book and write your review on Amazon.com. Thank you!

ADDITIONAL INFORMATION:

For information on classes or workshops, JOIN website:

www.ancestorpaths.net
www.honor-ur-ancestors.com

Email:
ancestorpaths@aol.com

Questions?
732-309-2625

To my ancestors,
it's been a while since
i spoke to you. I'm utterly
disppointed in myself. I am so
sorry for everything that has happen.
I take full responsbility for this.
This book is for us. So I will learn
how to reconnect with you throught
this book. Please forgive me.

— Crystal Via
10/16/2023
@
1:31 Pm

Made in the USA
Coppell, TX
16 February 2023

12885145R00154